FORBIDDEN FEMININITY

In memory of Rory and Rusty

Forbidden Femininity

Child Sexual Abuse and Female Sexuality

COLIN CRAWFORD
Department of Applied Social Studies
University of Ulster at Jordanstown
Analytical Psychotherapist

Ashgate

Aldershot • Brookfield USA • Singapore • Sydney

Published by
Ashgate Publishing Limited
Gower House
Croft Road
Aldershot
Hants GU11 3HR
England

Ashgate Publishing Company
Old Post Road
Brookfield
Vermont 05036
USA

British Library Cataloguing in Publication Data

Crawford, Colin
    Forbidden femininity : child sexual abuse and female
    sexuality
    1. Femininity (Psychology) 2. Women - Sexual behaviour 3. Child
    sexual abuse
    I. Title
    306.7 ' 082

Library of Congress Catalog Card Number: 97-72665

ISBN 1 85972 679 8

Printed and bound by Athenaeum Press, Ltd.,
Gateshead, Tyne & Wear.

Contents

Tables

Acknowledgements

In presenting this study I would wish to acknowledge the invaluable contributions derived from the work and research of Sigmund Freud, Louise Kaplin, Michele Elliot, Nancy Friday, Estela Welldon, Sue Lees, Ian Gibson et al. I should also wish to thank those psychiatrists and psychotherapists who co-operated in the research. Equally, however, I should like to pay tribute to the various respondents as quoted in Nancy Friday's and Michelle Elliot's work. They provide for unique source material relating to both female fantasy, and abuse, which no doubt will be further examined in subsequent research.

My sincere thanks also to Ruth Tovey who converted the chaos of my notes into the order of this manuscript.

My thanks also to Mary Anderson and Professor David Bamford for their editorial assistance in the production of the manuscript.

And finally to Gillian, for being there.

Preface

"And now we are struck by the significance of the possibility that the aggressiveness may not be able to find satisfaction in the external world because it comes up against real obstacles. If this happens, it will perhaps retreat and increase the amount of self-destructiveness holding sway in the interior ... Impeded aggressiveness seems to involve grave injury."

Freud, S (1975) *New Introductory Lectures on Psychoanalysis and Other Works, Anxiety and Instinctual Life*, Vol. XXII, (1932-36) Ed. J. Strachey et al, Hogarth Press, London. p.105.

Introduction

This study has attempted to draw upon, and contextualise, themes of female sexuality as identified in academic,[1] literary,[2] research,[3] and popular publications.[4] In particular this work examines: A The reality of maternal sexuality, upon the basis of Freudian, and other literature.[5] B The socially required suppression of female sexuality.[6] C Clinical case histories, which suggest the expression of a sadistic impulse in female abusing and sexual abuse complimented by survivors accounts.[7] D Accounts of maternal sexuality, as derived from empirical research.[8] E The realities of female sexuality, as evidenced in accounts of feminine sexual fantasy.[9] F The prevalence and nature of female sexual abuse, as derived from the literature, research, and survivor's accounts.[10]

As the material presented substantially contradicts our socially informed view of the feminine and the maternal, the final chapter considers one metapsychological approach which may have application in understanding the paradox of feminine sexuality.

Our perception of reality is centrally influenced by what we want and need to see, and believe. The problem is that what we, the social collective, want and need to see and believe, is not necessarily the truth. Indeed there may well be an imperative, individually and collectively, to protect ourselves from the primitive realities which constitute the true state of affairs within the human condition. This is most abundantly apparent in social and cultural attitudes toward human sexuality, where propriety and regulation abound.[11] Infantile sexuality is discouraged in expression, and not uncommonly punished. Girls who are openly sexual are termed promiscuous, "slags and sluts". Male homosexuals are called "queers", female homosexuals are labelled "gays" and "dykes".[12] Marital infidelity is viewed as morally wrong and corrupt as it detracts from a vision of marital happiness. Some religious orders take the view that sex, if not for procreation, is sinful. These are enormously powerful inhibitors to any sense of freedom in sexual identity and expression, which are socialised into, and internalised by us. However the sexual taboos, proscriptions and attitudes are there, arguably, to protect us from ourselves, in the interests of the society and the culture.[13] Our true sexuality, the libidinal essence of who we are may be accordingly sacrificed, or repressed out of consciousness, that we may act out the emasculated versions of sexuality, that are assigned to us. It is as if we must defend ourselves from the sexual drives, impulses and fantasies we experience in the "internal world", as these are personally (because we have internalised the proscription, and apply it to ourselves) socially and culturally unacceptable. [14]

This work challenges the social and cultural view and expectations of female sexuality. While we have the stereotypical archetypes of the feminine, maternal, nurturing woman, these are derived more from social constructions, than from a psychopathological reality.[15] Indeed the passive, maternal, facade, or projection of the feminine self, may be designed to defend against a darker and more primitive internal reality.[16] Accordingly projected passivity may defend against aggressive impulses, and pure maternalism, against a deep sexuality which may extend to "perverse motherhood".[17] Conversely male assertiveness, aggression and sexual primacy may be seen as defensive positions against passive/dependant tendencies, and relative sexual inferiority. In this paradox femininity may be viewed as a "persona system" employed to defend against "masculine" impulses of aggressive sexuality, and the exploration of the full parameters of true female sexuality.

While we have the social notion of the sexually aggressive male, and the passive female, the reality is that the male is capable, at the extreme, of seven orgasms in one hour, the female capacity is over one hundred. Further, the heartbeat of the female at the point of orgasm is higher than that of the male. This would suggest that the female has a much greater sexual capacity, and potentiality, than the male, However this is a reality which contradicts the demands of both gender stereotype, and the prevailing culture[18] Accordingly a conflict may arise between a woman's wish to indulge the full range of the internally experienced sexual impulses, and social expectations which require conformity to a stereotype of passive femininity.[19] In such circumstances of conflict, socialisation, repression, and internalised proscription, normally ensures the ascendancy of female virtuosity over female sexuality. The social expectations, and demands, for female virtuosity clearly extend to motherhood, and virtuous maternalism. [20]

The maternal aspect of femininity does involve a disposition of love, and "primary maternal pre-occupation". However the parameters of maternalism also extend to dominance, control, training, discipline, which can clearly be associated with the masculine and the potentially sadistic.

As this is inconsistent with the stereotype of femininity, it may be the reluctant father who is assigned the role of physical discipline and punishment. Indeed this is not uncommonly the case. However, this may actually represent an extension of female power and control, involving both the father, and child, which masks the sadistic impulse of the female, in a way which is socially acceptable. With regard to control and power in relationships, it is interesting to note the Freudian observation, that a wife is never happy until she has succeeded in turning her husband into her child. That is to say, until she has achieved a position of dominance and control in relation to him.[21] This can be readily observed in social and marital relations were women often actually occupy a position of dominance and control. However there is a tendency to mask this reality for public consumption,

2

where the husband (lover or partner) is "given his place". Equally it may be contended that the passive, gentle, unassertive stereotype of female sexuality may be a social, and socialised construct to defend against an internal or actual sexual reality. This sexual reality involves the dominant and sadistic impulse experienced, consciously or unconsciously by women. Where the impulse is repressed, this may give rise to neuroticism and apparent irrationality in women. It may be that the demands of civilisation and culture preclude the expression of the masculine (aggressive/sadistic) impulse experienced (consciously or unconsciously) by women, necessitating its affective discharge perversely, or symptomatically. (Depression, anxiety, panic attacks, phobias, neuroticism). This study attempts to explore the parameters of female sexuality, extending to examine female sexual abuse and perversion.[22] It is contended that the analysis of such pathological behaviours holds the key to understanding impulses and strivings central to "femininity", which may ordinarily exist, beneath the veneer of a socially required and enforced repression.[23]

Notes

1   Freud, S. (1975) *New Introductory Lectures of Psychotherapy and Other Works:*   Femininity Vol XXII (1932-36) Ed. J. Strachey et al, Hogarth Press, London.
2   Beauvoir, S. de. (1972) *The Second Sex*, translated and edited by H M Ponshley, Penguin, London
3   Glaser, D. and Fiosh, S. (1980) *Child Sexual Abuse,* Macmillan, London.
4   Friday, N. (1991) *Women on Top,* B C A, London
5   Freud, S. (1975) *A Case of Hysteria, Three Essays on Sexuality and Other Works.* Vol. VII (1901-05) Ed. J. Strachey et al, Hogarth Press, London.
6   Elliott, M. (19921) *Female Sexual Abuse of Children the ultimate Taboo,* Longman, Essex.
7   Finkelhor, D., Williams, L., Burns, N., (1988) *Nursery Crimes. Sexual Abuse in Day Care,* Sage, California.
8   Ibid.
9   Friday, op. cit.
10   Elliot, op. cit.
11   Bloch, I. (1938) *Sexual Life in England Past and Present,* London.
12   Lees, S. (1993) *Sugar and Spice, Sexuality and Adolescent Girls,* Penquin, London.
13   Freud, S. (1975) *Totem and Taboo and Other Works* , Ed.J Strachey et al, Vol. XIII (1913-14), Hogarth Press, London
14   Freud, S. (1975) *Totem and Taboo,* op. cit.
15   Weldon, C. V., (1988) *Mother Madonna Whore. The Idealisation and Denegration of Motherhood.* Free Association Books, London.
16   Ibid.
17   Ibid.
18   Lees, op. cit.

19   Lees, op. cit.
20   Weldon, op. cit.
21   Freud, S. (1975) *New Introductory Lecturess:* Femininity, op. cit.
22   Kaplan, L. (1991) *Female Perversions,* Penquin, London.
23   Ibid.

1 The Freudian context

Freud's seduction theory [1] explored and exposed the highly sensitive realities of infantile and childhood sexuality. [2] For a number of reasons, which will be considered in detail, he chose to re-evaluate his original contention, which pointed to pervasive child sexual abuse. [3] This was subsequently characterised as his female patients, libidinal or sexual, fantasised desire for their fathers. [4] This presents as a remarkable change in the theoretical conceptualisation of the problem, which informed the subsequent treatment of his hysterical female patients. There is an abundance of evidence to support the view that children do fantasise about, and do desire sexual contact with their parents, which was substantiated by Freud, at the cost of "social outrage". [5] Freud's social and professional audience were perhaps stretched enough by this revelation, without having to contend with the exposure of prevalent child sexual abuse in what was regarded as a highly civilised society. [6] Clearly there would have been enormous political, professional, cultural and personal pressures upon Freud in revising his original contention, and in his reaching more personally and socially circumspect conclusion. That is, to place an alternative explanatory construction on what were presented testimonies of child sex abuse, to characterise them as fantasised desires, and thus evade the devastating conclusions.

It was precisely these discoveries of childhood seductions which led to Breuer's terminating his association with Freud in 1894. Freud later observed,

> When I began more and more resolutely to put forward the significance of sexuality in the aetiology of the neuroses (Breuer) was the first to show the reaction of distaste and repudiation which was later to become so familiar to me, but which at that time I had not yet learned to recognise my inevitable fate. [7]

As a result Freud may have become particularly sensitive to the political, social, and professional responses toward, and consequences of, his findings. While the revelation of child sexuality was outrageous, implying the existence of a reciprocal sexual tendency in mothers, toward their children would have constituted the grounds for social and professional suicide. However he established that infants and children's "interest in sex can reach pathological intensity",[8] and that "we find the 'fantasy' of seduction once more in the pre-Oedipus pre-history of girls, but the seducer is regularly the mother".[9] And that further to this "it was the mother who by her activities over the child's bodily hygiene inevitably stimulated, and perhaps even roused for the first times pleasurable sensations in her genitals".[10] Clearly in this sentence Freud was making a politically sensitive distinction between stimulate and rouse, one definition of which is to provoke to activity. That this happens is undeniable. "Nursemaids have fondled the genital organs of their charges, mothers have caressed their sons and daughters sexually as well as maternally".[11] Freud also encountered instances of female/child sexual abuse within the ranks of the medical profession.

> When I first made enquiries about what was known on the subject, I learned from colleagues that there are several publications by paediatricians which stigmatise the frequency of sexual practices by nurses, and nursery maids, carried out even on infants in arms. [12]

In his discussion of the specific aetiology of hysteria Freud focused upon the effects caused by early trauma "which must be sexual".[13] He stated "the trauma has to be passively experienced and must consist of an 'actual imitation of the genitals' (of processes resembling copulation)".[14] He further observed that it was "usually an adult - a relative sometimes the father in the case of female hysterics, who seem to be more numerous than males - is the instigator".[15] For boys, "nursemaids, governesses, and domestic servants were frequently implicated".[16] The fact that mothers, the primary carer, the external object (that) "makes it possible to refine crude instincts into organised, pleasure principle, sophisticated needs that involve expressed sexuality, sensual and aesthetic feelings",[17] are not implicated, appears to be a gentlemanly, but none the less remarkable omission. It could be argued that mothers may have a constitutional, and instinctually directed developmental/transitional function in this regard, meeting to a greater or lesser degree the sensual and sexual demands of their children. As Freud observes,

> This is especially true since the person who is in charge of him, who, after all is as a rule his mother, herself regards him with feelings that are derived from her own sexual life; she strokes him kisses him, rocks him and quite clearly treats him as a substitute for a complete sex object.... What we call affection will unfailingly shows its effects one day on the genital zones as well. [18]

Not untypically, this was a revolutionary observation. The implications which it carries have been crucially neglected in theoretical understanding, research and professional practice. The underlying assumption has a relevance not only for the points which will be made in this paper, but for its entire philosophical ethos. That is to say that women experience an impulse toward "maternal sexuality" and that, not uncommonly, they act it out. Alternatively the impulse may be 'repressed out of consciousness', in which case it will create psychical conflict finding expression symptomatically, typically in neuroticism. It is implicitly and explicitly contended in this paper that "maternal sexuality" pervades all aspects of female sexuality and erotic life. Clearly there are degrees of sexual involvement which may be taken close to or beyond a sexual or abusing relationship per se. The realities of infantile sexuality, as a secretive dimension of nurture, subsequently become inaccessible to conscious recall, under "oedipal amnesia".[19] However social and even legal prescription abound in this most sensitive arena of infantile and childhood development involving the primary, most formative and significant of all human relationships. As Freud observes,

> It has become our habit to say that civilisation has been built up and the cost of sexual trends which, being inhibited by society, are partly, it is true, repressed but have partly been made usable for other aims". It is not easy for us to fulfil the requirements of this civilisation or to feel comfortable in it, because the instinctual restrictions imposed on us constitute a heavy psychical burden....[20]

This may be seen as a further factor disposing woman to relative neuroticism, in addition to those as outlined by Freud in his "Femininity" lecture.[21]

During the past twenty years, and particularly since the reorganisation of the Personal Health and Social Services under Seebohm and the Children's Order 1996, social workers have been extensively and increasingly involved in work with children and families.[22] This has been one of the principle factors around the 're-exposure' of the prevalence of child sex abuse (as opposed to child sexuality), however this time, for better or worse, it has been acted upon. For better or worse is an interesting theme which is the subject of contemporary debate. Perhaps when Freud was giving his original consideration to exposing the realities of child "sexual abuse", his insight led to the conclusion that acting against child sex abuse would have more destructive consequences, than acknowledging and tolerating it. In any case the social structures and child care provision at that period would have been wholly inadequate in dealing with the problem.

Contemporary responses to child sex abuse are arguably draconian and potentially highly destructive, particularly for the children involved. Social workers working in child care teams, residential units, training schools, etc, are well aware of this, but are compelled into action through statutory and legal obligation.[23]   Many children placed in care went on to become sexually abused in childrens' homes, or by their foster parents. At times such sexual abuse was both highly organised and systematic, and not uncommonly this involved homosexual abuse. Many children who were removed from home and placed in care, inform us that their lives were ruined as a result of benign social services intervention. It would appear that the statutory regulation of child/adult sexuality is more located in maintaining and policing a moral taboo, than in childrens' or family welfare. And yet we know that the prevalence of child sex abuse is so extensive as to render it a cultural norm in certain sections of society. Some writers are suggesting, controversially, that children are not damaged by consensual sexual relationships with their parents. They also contend, correctly in my view, that the problem is not just located in child/adult sexual relationships within families, but in the subsequent social, professional and legal responses toward it. (Stigma, labelling, status passage, victimisation, mortification, imprisonment, reception into 'care', etc).

There are complementary tendencies in the realm of parent child emotional, and sexual attachments. The incest taboo exists precisely to prohibit the primal/constitutional impulse to have sexual relations with one's children. However, children continue to powerfully evidence this sexual attractedness, being, by definition, free from the social and moral proscription influencing to a greater or lesser degree their parents. Freud established infantile and childhood sexual desire for parents; and the existence of a reciprocal adult sexual desire for children (that is, adult sexual desires responsively complementing childhood sexual desire). This has particular implications for the early maternal relationships, to be considered in this paper.

Research evidence suggests a pervasive incidence of male sexual abuse of children. A significant and increasing percentage of our prison population are male sex offenders. Until recently this was regarded as "the last taboo". However there is increasing evidence to suggest "sexual abuse" of children by mothers and females may also be highly prevalent.

While literary and research data will be presented to support this view, the findings of Bagley and Young (1988) serves to place this theme in context. "Twenty-four per cent of women aged 22 to 36, in a survey of 632 mothers with young children reported sexual abuse involving at least contact with their (the mother's) genital area, before age 17". This would appear to support Freud's view that "an innate incest" desire is evident in early childhood and that it continues throughout life in a repressed form". [24] However, Bagley and Young's research would indicate that this is increasingly finding expression between mothers and their children. Freud interpreted many of his clinical cases as indicating a strong incest desire in children and adults, and more recent clinical writings have also emphasised the presence of a strong incest desire. [25] Lindzey agreed with the Freudian concept of an incest taboo and was instrumental in resurrecting the theory that this had a biological basis. [26] However, an alternative view can be advanced, that it is "the universality and continued strength of the incest taboo (that) suggests that there is a strong incest desire". [27]

Notes

1   Freud, S. (1975) *Three Essays on the Theory of Sexuality Vol. VII (1911-13)* Ed. Strachey, J. et al, Hogarth Press, London, pp. 124-245.
2   Ibid, p. 36.
3   Freud, S. (1975) *New Introductory Lectures Vol. XXII (1936)* Ed Strachey, J. et al, Hogarth Press, London.
        See Stevens, R. (1983) *Freud and Psychoanalysis*, An Exposition and Appraisal. Open University Press, Milton Keynes, p. 57.

Also Brown, D. and Pedder, J. (1991) *Introduction to Psychotherapy*, Routledge, London, p. 33.

4   Stevens, R. op. cit. p. 57.

5   Brown, D. and Pedder, J. op. cit. p.33.
     Kline, P. (1984) *Psychology and Freudian Theory*, Methuen, London, p. 44.
     Also Storr, A. (1989) *Freud*, Oxford University Press, Oxford, p.18.

6   Jahoda, M. (1977) *Freud and the Dilemmas of Psychology*, Hogarth Press, London.

7   Freud, S. (1975) *Pre-psychoanalytic Publications and Unpublished Draft* (1886-89) Ed. Strachey, J. et al, Hogarth Press, London.

8   Giovacchini, P. (1982) *A Clinicians Guide to Reading Freud*, Aronson, New York, p. 115.

9   Freud, S. *New Introductory Lectures*, op. cit. p. 120.

10   Freud, S. *New Introductory Lectures*, op. cit. p. 120.

11   Giovacchini, P. (Further remarks on the defence of the neuro-psychoses) op. cit.

12   Freud, S. (1975) *Early Psychoanalytic Publications* Vol. III (1893-99), Ed. Strachey, J. et al, Hogarth Press, London.

13   Ibid, p. 163-164.

14   Ibid, p.163.

15   Ibid, p.164.

16   Ibid, p.164.

17   Freud, S. (1975) *Three Essays on Sexuality and other Works* Vol. VII (1901-1905) Ed. Strachey, J. et. al., Hogarth Press, London, p. 223.

18   Freud, S. *Early Psychoanalytic Publications*, op. cit. p. 207.

19   Freud, S. *New Introductory Lectures*, op. cit. p. 110.

20   Ibid, p. 110.

21   Ibid, pp. 127-135

22   Seebohm Report (1968) Report of the Committees on Local Authority and Allied Personal Social Services Cmnd 3703, HMSO London.
     Also New Childrens Order (1996) HMSO London.

23   Leedings *Child Care Manual for Social Workers* (1982) Butterworths, London, pp. 67-103.

24   Meiselman, K. (1979) Incest. *A Psychological Study of Causes and Effects with Treatment Recommendations*, Jersey Bass, London. pp. 8-9.

25   Ibid, pp. 1-27.

26   Lindzey, B. (1967) Some Remarks Concerning Incest, the Incest Taboo and Psychological Theory, *American Psychologist,* 22, pp. 1051-1059.

27   Freud, S. (1975) *Totem and Taboo and other Works*, Vol. XIII (1913-14) Ed. Strachey, J. et al, Hogarth Press, London.

2 The social and internal pathology of female sexuality

The true nature of female sexuality remains obscure, subject as it is to repression and social sanction. In stark contrast male sexuality is comparatively acceptable, and understood. Sex, and the management of sexuality in public and in society, is an enormously powerful theme which can centrally determine how we live and in very extreme circumstances how we die. Islamic society provides us with a draconian model of the regulation of sexual propriety in society. A British Parliamentary Human Rights Group presented disturbing findings relating to the treatment of Iranian women under the Mullahs (1994).

> The M.P.'s say that Iranian women are treated by the regime as subhuman, and that the law - which demands the death penalty for adultery and for women failing to cover themselves from head to foot - is routinely enforced in practice.

> The penalty for adultery is flogging for an unmarried man, but stoning to death for an unmarried woman.[1]

The article went on to make a further perverse link between sexuality and punishment. A former prison interrogator reported "virgin women must as a rule be raped before execution".[2]

The human rights group went on to give an account of a 53 year old woman's experience, whose offence was allowing her headscarf to slip from her forehead. (She did not have time to adjust it prior to her arrest). [3]

> Each of the women (aged between 15 and 62) was sentenced to receive 80 lashes. The women were herded into a basement by the guards. One was holding a whip in his hand. They handcuffed me face down on a wooden bed...then they started whipping me. What they did to me hurt more mentally I think than physically...the lack of power, being robbed of all dignity. "The number of women who take their own lives bears testimony

to the misery they endure".[4] (2,530 women committed suicide in Khorasan province alone, during 1993). [5]

While these particular responses to sexuality, and female sexuality in particular, are characteristic of a primitive and brutal society, the underlying imperative toward female morality is evident in all societies.[6] Ironically, in contemporary society, its enforcement is policed, not principally by men, but by female peers who may speak of sexual emancipation, while serving the cause of repression, and demanding conformity in sexual propriety.[7] Clearly this gives rise to the central conflict experienced by most women between their true sexuality (as evidenced in the "internal world") with sexual impulses and instinctual libidinal drives, and the contradictory social expectations of women, as demanded by peers, family, men and ultimately other women. At the extreme the expectations of sexual morality can be internalised to a point where frigidity is a consequence.[8] In short a majority of women experience sexual entrapment.[9] An implication deriving from this would suggest that female sexuality may be experienced more poignantly in the internal world, through fantasy, than in the external world, where the expression and enactment of their (initially experienced) sexuality may be responded to prescriptively. [10] Accordingly it will be necessary to review the restricted literature of female sexual fantasy at a later point, to explore the gulf between sexuality as experienced in the internal world, relative to the prohibitions and expectations of the external world.[11] While western civilization does not advocate stoning women to death, or beating them into compliant submission regarding the negation and self inflicted abandonment of their sexuality, socially contrived pressures and attitudinal proscription can be very effective in attaining a similar outcome.[12] (It is interesting that psychotherapy is one of the few treatment, or relationship mechanisms, which offers women the unrestricted opportunity to share their experienced sexuality fantasies, desires, obsessions and perversions. It is hardly surprising that this intimate relationship is often erotically charged both in terms of content and affect).[13]

The medical profession have historically represented the interests of sexual morality and propriety (although whether this is a defence against their own experienced sexuality is debatable, i.e., "some doctors may have tried to avoid making a vaginal examination of any sort except in the most pressing cases").[14]

They could find men's and women's admissions about irregular sexual habits 'disgusting', 'sickening', and 'repulsive', something it was 'natural' to want to ignore, or at least a regrettable necessity of their work which was 'debasing in its tendencies' and called for strong principles in ourselves. Some felt that it would be right to err on the side of severity about masturbation even if its harmful effects were in doubt. [15]

Even Freud reflected the moral attitudes of his medical contemporaries, which are in certain sections of the profession still in evidence today.

A girl suffered from obsessional self-reproaches.

Close questioning then revealed the source from which her guilt arose. Stimulated by a chance voluptuous sensation, she had allowed herself to be led astray by a woman friend to masturbating and had practised it for years, fully conscious of her wrong doing....A few months after treatment and the strictest surveillance, the girl recovered.[16]

A separate account continued the theme.

A girl reproached herself for things she knew were absurd...She reproached herself with the masturbation she had been practising in secret without being able to renounce it. She was cured by careful surveillance which prevented her from masturbating.[17]

The 'medicalisation' of sexuality, and female sexuality in particular, has historically veiled a morally inspired punitive desire for its eradication.

Belief in a pathology of female masturbation was more current in higher levels of the profession"...Many specialists seem to have believed that nervous disorders in women, ranging from epilepsy to schizophrenia, were due to masturbation.[18]

Tissot left us in no doubt as to the adverse effects of masturbation, which carried a greater symptomatic consequences for women.[19]

Onanism (masturbation) affected females in the same way as males but in addition caused them to be subject to hysterical fits, incurable jaundice, violent cramps in the stomach, pains in the nose, ulceration of the matrix, and uterine tremors, which deprived them of decency and reason and lowered them to the level of the most lascivious, vicious brutes... Onanism was particularly debilitating to those who had not yet attained puberty, because it tended to destroy the mental faculties by putting too great a strain on the nervous system.[20]

Accordingly Tissot made his contribution to the 'scientific' understanding of human, and specifically female sexuality, which was to inform medical opinion significantly, for decades. Kitchener makes a similar contribution, if less diplomatically, to our understanding of female sexuality, extending somewhat the consequence of malady ensuing the self-stimulation of the female genitalia.[21]

Women masturbators not only suffered from the consequences that males did but also were afflicted with rickets, hysteria, jaundice, stomach cramps, womb ulcers, elongation and eruption of the clitoris, juror uterinus, loss of interest in the opposite sex, hermaphoclitism, leucorrhea, painful menstruation, falling of the womb, loss of pleasure in the sex act, painful childbirth, and obstinate sterility.[22]

All of this really indicated a pathological fear and loathing of the sexual, and sexuality, with a particular application to women. It appeared that female sexuality, and any expression of the libidinal impulse by women, had to be eradicated in the interests of the prevailing moral order. Complementing this there appeared to be a gender conspiracy culminating in a collective denial of psychically experienced sexuality.

> For many writers, the woman who enjoyed sex was a sick creature, and women themselves tended to agree... Some of the strongest advocates of women's maternal nature, were other women.[23]

Obsessional defences against sexuality were barbaric and very evident in America.

> With such attitudes toward the dangers of sexual abuse (i.e., masturbation), there was a determined effort to find preventatives for those 'unable' to 'control' their own sexuality. Some doctors perforated the foreskin of the penis and inserted a ring or cut the foreskin with jagged scissors. Others applied ointment that would make the genitals tender to touch, and others applied hot irons to girls thighs. In some cases clitoridectomies were performed, and in a few cases actual amputation of the penis was attempted to prevent masturbation. Castration was not uncommon. Most popular. however, were the mechanical devices that the interested could purchase: large numbers of these are listed under the category of medical appliances in US Patent Office records. There were various kinds of devices with metal teeth designed to prevent erection in the male, or various kinds of guards to be worn around the pudenda of the female. [24]

In France to such devices were advertised in national newspapers. [25]
In his writings Freud comments

> The analysis of cases in which circumcision, thought not it is true, castration, has been carried out on boys as a cure or punishment for masturbation (a far from rare occurrence in Anglo American Society) has given our conviction at last a degree of certainty (i.e., the castration complex).[26]

However it is, as always, the management of female sexuality which attracts particular attention and intervention in many societies. This can involve the literal desexualisation of women through genital mutilation (already mentioned in relation to America). What the medical profession tried to achieve by threat of consequence (i.e., of masturbation) others (including doctors) achieve through the surgical destruction of the female genital organs. It was estimated in 1979 that some 20 million women had been subjected to such mutilation.[27]

> Genital mutilation is an inhuman torture used to ensure chastity in which the primary source of female eroticism is surgically removed by the midwife priest or doctor....

Besides ensuring chastity, infibulation has now another function. According to Esther Ogunmodede of Now-Nigerian Organisation for Woman, the narrow opening which results after the wound has healed increases the husband's pleasurable sensations during intercourse, even though for the women, sex is nothing but agony, one reason why she does not bother to take a lover. [28]

> ....These rituals are usually performed at puberty. In some cases the women has to be opened for sexual intercourse and childbirth after marriage. [29]

Such interventions are clearly both barbaric and horrific, however punitive social attitudes and a "required" rejection of sexuality, which may be internalised and converted in responses of guilt and self rejection, are equally as damaging. At the extreme there may be a distinct similarity of consequences. The incidence of child sexual abuse carried out, or sanitised under the guise of sexual "morality" was truly remarkable. Once again it was women who feature prominently in the erotic and perverse "moral" management of infantile sexuality.

> Masturbation was a never ending source of inspiration. At night the child was chained or strapped or handcuffed to his or her bed so that all body movement was rendered impossible. During the day the lower part of the child's body could be locked into metal contraptions that served as underwear. Wealthy parents instructed the governesses and tutors to whom they entrusted their children that they should take any measure necessary to ensure sexual straightness. It was not uncommon for children to be sexually stimulated by their governesses and then bound up in leather straps or chains to ensure that they would not masturbate. Like a true saint the child was tempted into desire then humiliated into tormenting renunciation... [30]

An explanatory construction for this is quite straightforward. Sexuality has to be punished, and the punishment of sexuality is erotically or perversely sexual.

As Stekal implied in his paper Sadism and Masochism, there is no cruelty not tinged with sexual pleasure. [31] "Medicalised perversion" would have given greater cause for concern.

> Physicians turned their attention from mild cures to methods of total suppression. Restraining devices, severe punishments and surgery were among the reputable cures... For winding around the unruly penis were all manners of mechanical devices of rubber, wire, and springs. Catheters and tubes could be inserted within the penis... Clitoridectomy, a cure that removed the offending organ, was, mercifully, a brief fad. Nevertheless, blistering of the thighs and genitals, "burial" of the clitoris beneath the labia, cauterisation, and infibulation of the labia majora were frequently recommended. [32]

The crucially obvious consequence of these interventions however would have been the creation, or amplification, of an obsession with sexuality, which as a direct consequence of its perverse management in infancy, would find perverse expression in adulthood. The most likely target for the application of such acquired perversions would be children, carrying an intergenerational implication for both the acquisition and expression of, perversion, and specifically the perversion of child sexual abuse. In this regard women are as likely as men to manifest the 'compulsion to repeat' personally experienced sexual abuse in the past, with children in the present. Indeed if opportunity is an important variable in the incidence of perverse child sexual abuse, women are much more likely to be so involved. Ironically women would derive a real protection in this regard, from societal attitudes which enshrines - despite any presented realities - feminine virtuosity, and maternal sacrosanctity, in which cause, after all, perversion may be enacted. The apparent quest for purity and asexuality in the maternal management of childhood, actually provided opportunities for erotic perversion.

> Companies made fortunes on the sale of electric belts and suspension apparatuses, many of which awakened even more exotic erotic fantasies than the child or adolescent could have conjured on his (or her) own and thereby stimulated more elaborate methods or onanism (masturbation).[33]

A symbolic interactionist analysis of perverse erotic interventions with sexually active children points to the certainty of dysfunctional outcome achieved.

The labelling thesis contends that societal responses to deviance have the opposite to the intended effect: that they are dysfunctional, that negative responses actually have a stimulus effect. That defining people as "deviant", or "sexually deviant", and subsequently treating them as outsiders (those having offended against a moral code), leads people so designated into further deviation. The labelling perspective reversed comparatively traditional ways of conceptualising offending and identified the deviant as the victim, the subject of projections, stimulating deviancy.

> The person becomes the thing he is described as being. Nor does it seem to matter whether the valuation is made by those who would punish or by those who would reform. The parents or the policemen, the older brother or the court, the probation officer or the juvenile institutions in so far as they rest upon the thing complained of, rest upon a false ground. Their very enthusiasm defeats their aim. The harder they work to reform the evil, the greater the evil grows in their hands.[34]

Central to the labelling thesis is the notion of the self fulfilling prophecy, and the social construction of reality,

> The process of making the criminal (or sexual "offender" or "pervert") therefore, is a process of tagging, defining, identifying, segregating, describing, emphasising, making conscious and self conscious, it becomes

a way of stimulating, suggesting emphasising, and evoking the very traits complained of...The person becomes the thing he is described as being.[35]

This view identifies society, or the regulations of the sexual morality, as the deviancy processors, labellers, stigmatisers, and victimisers, presenting the deviant as victim.

All social groups make rules and attempt at some times and under some circumstances, to enforce them. Social rules define situations and the kinds of behaviour appropriate to them, specifying some actions as "right" and forbidding others as "wrong". When a rule is enforced the person who is supposed to have broken it may be seen as a special kind of person, one who cannot be trusted to live by the rules agreed on by the group. He is regarded as an outsider.[36]

Becker's approach focused on societal reaction to deviance (in this case sexual deviation) which he viewed as dysfunctional. The individual identified as deviant, processed by control agencies, made the subject of degradation ceremonies, typed, institutionalised, imprisoned, in short stigmatised.[37] Further to this Becker contended that the new ascribed or designated status constituted a "master status", with implications for the individual extending beyond his original "offending" behaviour, to all aspects of his "moral character".[38] That social perceptions of the individual as "bad" or "perverted" in one respect had commensurate connotations for all respects of his behaviour.[39]

Adopting a more sophisticated approach Lemert differentiated between "primary deviance", arising from situational, circumstantial, cultural, psychological factors, and "secondary deviance" involving societal response, designation and labelling.[40] Lemert contended that the labelling process, involving status transformation in terms of audience, carried commensurate psychic implications for the individual so typed.[41] Accordingly the labelling and perverse treatment of the child, male or female, as a sexual deviant or pervert, ensured precisely that consequence.

Other sociological perspectives have an equally interesting application in considering the creation and amplification of sexual perversion; Sutherland and Cressey, Learning and Transmitting Criminal Behaviour;[42] Cloward and Ohlin, Delinquency and Opportunity;[43] Hawkins and Tiedeman, The Creation of Deviance;[44] Sutherland and Cressey, Differential Association;[45] Durkheim, Anomie Theory.[46]

In the social management of sexuality there is evidence to support the view that women themselves tend to conspire in their own sexual repression, and entrapment. Even the possibilities of friendship are constrained through "sexual politics".

Rarely rising to genuine friendship...as they all face together the masculine world, whose values they wish to monopolise each for her self...And so in the sphere of coquetry and love each woman sees in every other an enemy.[47]

In a similar vein Woolf observes

> So often women are not seen by the other sex, but only in relation to the other sex. So common sense even dictates that women are not really capable of friendship - or at least real friendship. [48]

Gender management and gender acculturation are highly evident in all aspects of socialisation and education, and this is internalised, in such a way, and with such force that girls themselves become the carriers of the culture of their own oppression. This phenomenon has a relationship to a "collective identification with the aggressor", the "aggressor" being the points of human contact which demand conformity to their expectations of the feminine stereotype. In what is a subtle and all pervasive process, initial rebellion, may be responded to, externally, through a withdrawal of affection, expressed trust, and rejection, amplifying in the girl, an already implanted guilt, which is centrally targeted upon her sexual self and her sexuality. As we had masturbatory censure in infancy and childhood, and the implantation of guilt, the censure encountered in adolescence is managed socially, and sub-culturally. Sexuality is controlled even through female peer group pressure which demands conformity to notions of 'the feminine'. Language and labelling are the central mechanisms of sexual regulation, which may be extent to conferment of stigma (as slut, slag, whore, nympho, i.e., the designation of "bad" women), exclusion from the group specifically, or female company generally, and at the extreme, physical assault.

As one of Lees respondents comments,

> Why would you have defined the two girls as slags?

> - Because they were using people and became very flirtatious. You would recognise them as the same people. You could be having a conversation with them one minute. Someone they like comes into the room, suddenly they change their whole personalities. They don't talk to you sincerely. It's tits out. And then all they want with the boys is to get off with them. [49]

What would be seen as natural, expected and even encouraged within an ethos of masculinity, is social taboo for girls, creating conflicts once again between internal and external worlds. The socially contrived dichotomy between who they are, and the emotions they experience and wish to express, and who they are allowed to be, in the "real world". (Given their vulnerability to, and fear of, censure and disapproval).

Another account from Lee's work makes the point

> Laura describes the kind of episode that can occur:
> My friend knows this girl and she's a bit of a tart and she invites boys to her house and once these skinheads came along and she started taking her clothes off and everything and these boys said they didn't have any girlfriends but the girls were waiting outside and they brought their girlfriends in and beat her up and everything and she was in hospital, so

17

now no-one takes any notice of her or anything, they just leave her to herself...

What do you think about that?

- It was her own fault, she shouldn't do it - it's horrible.[50]

It is quite apparent from this account that the violent girl's own experienced sexuality, and 'vulnerability' to sexual 'acting out' was projected onto the victim, who was punished for enacting the scenario which they libidinally desired for themselves. This represents a fairly primitive attempt at "splitting off" the sexual, and punishing it, in effect distancing and sanitising themselves from a sexuality which threatens them. However, the central achievement here is the girls maintenance of their own sexual oppression.

As Lees comments,

> We have seen that the vocabulary used to describe girls divides them into the good and the bad, the promiscuous and the pure, the tasty and the 'dogs'. It is not only the boys that categorize girls in this way but girls use the same terms to categorize and 'police' each other. Embodied in their vocabulary is a contempt for women which emerges if they are seen to be actively sexual and unattached. What is particularly pernicious about this language is that it is accepted as part of nature, or of common sense, by the girls themselves.[51]

These contradictions of female identity are located crucially in the internal world, finding expression in the collective organisation of feminine or female society. The internalised association of guilt with sexuality, sexuality with punishment, and in punishment the expression of perverse sexuality. At its simplest, and most basic level, women tend to punish themselves, for libidinally experienced impulses, by discounting and negating their sexuality. They secondarily punish each other through, at times viciously, attacking signs and 'symptoms' of sexual 'liberation', indulgence or permissiveness. The motivation for this emanates from disallowing others (females) the expression of libidinally experienced "masculine" desires which they have suppressed or denied in themselves, at enormous psychical cost.

However the entire equation is centrally flawed, based as it is upon an anti-libidinal premise, and the consequences can be draconian. First we have the loss of the sexual self, through the enactment of super ego and external expectations, ultimately we can discern the loss of identity, the loss of self.

'Womanliness' and femininity, therefore, can be social mechanisms employed to distance women from their sexual commonality with men. The myth of feminine virtuosity may be employed as a perverse compensatory defence against forbidden masculine 'sexual' impulses and drives. Accordingly comparative, or actual frigidity, cloaks the 'masculine' sexual impulse, which is viciously and sadistically responded to (culturally and internally, through super ego function) to become transmuted and disguised as feminine virtuosity.

18

The internal (internalised) and socially regulated imperative of female virtuosity involves therefore, both the denial and structured abandonment of the experience of "masculine" sexuality, which is both forbidden to women and by women, essentially out of fear of social consequence.

And so the internally and culturally contrived paradox reaches its conclusion, the feminine denial of sexuality is converted to the denial of the "true self". The outcome is one of pathos, with tragic personal and interpersonal consequence. Sometimes 'true' femininity, and the libidinal abuse which marks its nature, may be sublimated, channelled into art or poetry. However the true pathos of this aesthetic transmutation lies in an acknowledgement of its loss (the loss of true femininity). The informed reader accordingly does not relate most directly with the words of the poem, but with the desolation of the writer whose words serve to connect us with her experience of human despair. As Roberts comments in his review of Marsh's, Rossetti,

> In Rossetti's case, the childhood was crucially that of a girl who had to be ruthlessly moulded, even in that apparently easy going family, into the constrained moral forms required by conventional femininity. Parts of herself that did not fit, seemingly masculine, and therefore unnatural, had to be repressed. These dead fragments of her psychie are brought back to brilliant life in her poems. Anger, greed, showing off, sexual desire, competitiveness could flourish there like rampant beasts in a fantastical garden, although their presence in life was hidden.[52]

As Kaplan insightfully and eloquently observes, initially in relation to Madame Bovary,

> Emma Bovary is always looking around herself trying to locate the sources of her misery. She is not able to look for herself within herself and so has no option but to search for who and what she is in a stereotype of femininity.

> There is, though, a potential within each individual woman to arrive at more tempered versions of womanhood, perhaps not so far from Emma's fleeting notion of happiness. What it takes is the not inconsiderable courage to question the various aspects of womanliness that we have come to take for granted as the woman we are. In this painful examination of the corruptions of our spirit it is also necessary to scrutinize the Faustian bargains we have made with the social world in which we live.

> Along the way toward growing into a normal and socially acceptable womanhood we leave many of our possible lives by the wayside. But they are still there haunting the life we have chosen to lead. Sometimes, like Emma Bovary, we will imagine that our real life is the life we did not lead. We sense nameless feelings coursing through our breast and wonder what they could be. For a woman now, as in Emma's day, to explore and express the fullness of her sexuality, her ambitious, her emotional and intellectual capacities, her social duties, would entail who knows what

19

risks and who knows what truly revolutionary alteration of the social conditions that demean and constrain her. Or she may go on trying to fit herself into the order of the world and therefore consign herself forever to the bondage of some stereotype of normal femininity - a perversion, if you will.[53]

However in this quotation Kaplan, as it were, externalises 'blame', in identifying the oppressive factors exclusively in the external, and not the internal world, which characterises feminine responses central to their entrapment. It is precisely the response of externalisation, locating blame within social organisation and structure, which gives rise to a perception of hopelessness, resignation and fatalism. The "revolutionary alteration" must begin internally, with a re-evaluation and reassessment of the developmental factors which confine and contribute to the denial of both the sexual, and the actual self. Individualised feminine "revolution" may or may not lead to a collective revolution, but certainly it must begin at that level.

We have seen that a denial of sexuality can, and arguably must, lead to its perverse expression. The feminine denial of sexuality and the need to punish manifestations of sexuality in themselves and others carries a particular significance for motherhood. The mother who is not confident with her own sexuality, and who experiences guilt, demanding a punishment of the self, is quite likely to respond punitively to expressed sexuality in her children. Responses to masturbation, as documented, may be draconian, and while these may not be carried to extremes in contemporary society, the guilt ridden and punitive attitudes remain. This, therefore, is the genesis of all sexual conflict and neuroticism. The infantile reality of sexuality, and the responses to that part of him or herself, as encountered in the external world. It is here that the vital connections are made between what is good and rewarded, and what is bad, and punished. It is here that the psychical constructions are made that a "good girl is non sexual" and that "bad girls are sexual". These very powerful associations leave a psychological, psychical or pathological legacy, towards what are perverse responses toward infantile sexuality, creating internal conflict which may have as its ultimate consequence, frigidity, neuroticism, anorexia or madness.

The role of the female, the maternal, in this gender typing is crucial, and central to the conspiracy aimed primarily at the feminine child. While it is accepted by most mothers that the boy will be "sexual", and that "virility of maleness" should be encouraged, no such concessions are available to female children, who are not expected to share the "masculine" attributes of sexuality. They are much more likely to be enforced into a role and model of asexual femininity, of virtuosity, of purity, at great cost to the libidinal self, which is to be punished, abandoned, if you like, cut off.

In this way it is women themselves who regulate the genesis of the destruction of the sexual, feminine self. While we do not indulge in the practice of female genital mutilation as practised is Nigeria and elsewhere, do we achieve a similar outcome through the 'gentler' process of gender socialisation, and 'soul murder'.

Notes

1   Observer: 11.12.94 Women Treated as Sub-Humam.
2   Ibid.
3   Ibid.
4   Ibid.
5   Ibid.
6   Freud, S. (1975) Vol XIII, *Totem and Taboo and Other Works,* Ed Strachey et al, Hogarth Press, London, p. 188.
7   See Lees, S. (1993) *Sugar and Spice, Sexuality and Adolescent Girls,* Penguin, London, p. 63.
8   Freud, S. (1975) Vol XXII, *New Introductory Lectures of Psychoanalysis and Other Works*, Ed Strachey et al, Hogarth Press, London, p. 126.
9   Ibid, p. 134.
10   Ibid, p. 123.
11   Ibid, p 149.
12   Kaplan, L. J.(1993) *Female Perversions*, Penguin, London, p. 453.
13   See Freud, A.(1968) *The Ego and Mechanisms of Defence*, Hogart Press, London, (Transference of Libidinal Impulses), p. 18/19.
        Also Clark, D. S. (1965) *What Freud Really Said*, Penguin, London, p. 4749.
        Also Stevens, R.(1983) *Freud and Psychoanalysis*, Open University Press, Milton Keynes, pp. 61/62.
        Also Badcock, C. (1988) *Essential Freud*, Blackwell, Londong, p. 190.
14   *Medical Times* 21, (1850) London.
15   Mason, M. (1994) *The Making of Victorian Sexuality*, Oxford University Press, Oxford, p. 181.
16   Freud, S. (1975) Vol m, *Early Psychoanalytical Publications*, Hogarth Press, London, p. 55.
17   Ibid, p. 76.
18   Mason, op. cit. p. 204/205.
19   Tissot, S. A. D.(1758) *Dissertatio de Febribue Bilbliois*, Lausannef Switzerland: Marci-Mic Bousquet.
20   Ibid.
21   Kitchener, A. T. (1812) *Letters on Marriage*, Vol I, Chapple, London.
22   Ibid, p. 49.
23   Bullough, V. L. (1976) *Sexual Variance in Society and History*, University of Chicago Press, Chicago, p. 548.
24   Ibid, p. 549.
25   See Kaplan, op. cit. p. 423.
26   Freud, *New Introductory Lectures*, op. cit. p.87.
27   Barry, K. *Female Sexual Slavery*, New York University Press, New York, p. 189.
28   Ibid, p. 190.
29   Ibid, p.190.
30   Kaplan, op. cit. p.423.

31 Stekel, W. *Sadism and Masochism. The Psychology of Hatred and Cruelty,* translated by Louis Brink Liveright, New York, Vol I, p. 31/32.

32 Kaplan, op. cit. p.424.

33 Kaplan, op. cit. p.424.

34 Becker, H. (1963) *Outsiders, Studies in the Sociology of Deviance,* Glencoe Free Press, New York.

35 Tannenbaum, F. (1938) *Crime and the Community,* Columbia University Press, New York, p. 20.

36 Ibid, p. 19, 20.

37 Becker, H. (1968) *The Other Side, Perspectives on Deviance,* New York Free Press, p.1.

38 Becker, H. *Outsiders,* op. cit. p.34.

39 Becker, H. *Outsiders,* op. cit.

40 Lemert, E. (1967) *Human Deviance,* Social Problems and Social Control, Prentice Hall, New York, p. 28.

41 Ibid.

42 Sutherland, E. and Cressey, D. (1974) in *Principles of Criminology,* 9th Ed, Lippincott, Philadelphiag.

43 Clonard, R. and Ohlin. (1960) *Delinquency and Opportunity,* The Free Press, New York.

44 Hawkins, J. (1975) Tiederman. *The Creation of Deviance,* Merrill, Colunbas, Ohio, p. 318.

45 Sutherland, E. and Cressey, D. (1971) *Learning and Transmitting Criminal Behaviour.* The Criminal in Society, Ed L Radzinowcz, M Wolfgang, Basic Books Inc, USA, p. 400/406.

46 Durkheim, E. (1964) *Division of Labour and Society,* Free Press of Glencoe, New York, Vol 3, p. 353-373.

47 Beauvoir, S. de. (1972) *The Second Sex,* translated and edited by H M Ponshley, Penguin, London, p. 558.

48 Woolf, V. (1929) *A Room of One's Own.* Harcourt.

49 Lees, op. cit. p.48/49.

50 Lees, op. cit. p.48/49.

51 Lees, op. cit. p.56.

52 Roberts, M. (1976) *Sunday Times Literary Review*

53 Kaplan, p. 528.

3 Female fantasy: The internal, erotic female world

Freud has suggested that in every dream there lies a concealed wish.[1] Dreams according to Freud, allow a form of internal expression to repressed and unconscious desires, wishes and impulses, too alarming to be allowed into waking consciousness.[2]

> Wishes arise from it which during sleep might find the entrance to consciousness open. If we were to know them we would be appalled, alike by their subject matter, their unrestraint, and indeed the mere possibility of their existence.[3]

Fantasy is a much more restrained phenomenon finding unrestricted entry into consciousness and mental exposition. However, while there may be a desire to enact the fantasy, as Freud commented there may be an associated moral reaction which prevents it. As Freud wrote in relation to children harbouring murderous thoughts toward their father, the rival for the mother's affections.

> Accordingly the mere hostile impulse against the father, the mere existence of a wishful fantasy of killing and devouring him, would have been enough to produce the moral reaction that created (totemism and) taboo.[4]

As a consequence, fantasy, while providing a forum for the psychical expression of libidinal impulse, may serve most effectively in blocking or impeding its expression in external reality. Fantasy in its turn may be regarded as a codified or psychically sanitised version of id dominated primal impulses and desires. These can be very primitive impulses, of a sadistic or masochistic orientation, which may or may not find expression in reality. However the existence of such impulses, albeit, at the level of fantasy, is significant. It could be suggested that fantasy involving sexual perversion, represents a latent sexual desire seeking discharge. Fantasy therefore may give expression to a sexual impulse, as a prelude to its enactment, given circumstantial or situational opportunity. This paper implicitly makes links between experienced female fantasy, and enacted female perversion, which is remarkably similar in its sadistic locatedness.

The existence, and the meaning of experienced female fantasy has been under-researched and under-estimated by the academic community. Female sexual fantasy does exist, it is relatively common, and it has a meaning which must be analysed and better understood.[5]

Upon the basis of my own clinical experience I have been the subject of female 'transference' fantasy. This has extended to patients fantasies of my being tied up, minutely bodily inspected, being made to stand naked in a corner, beaten with a cane, whipped "all over", bathed, "like a child", and being forced to masturbate "when I couldn't". These were recurrent themes which were the subject of fantasy, and dream content. They were critically important in understanding the sexual conflicts experienced by female patients, between their true internally experienced sexuality, and the external demands of femininity. In many cases a patient's level of disturbance would be determined by the strength of the usually sadistic sexual impulse, and the psychical forces employed in repressing it.

It is fairly apparent that fantasy is an extremely important mechanism in giving some expression to a sense of the sexual, and the erotic, which may be repressed and crushed out of the conscious possibility of actualisation - for most women. However the reality is that if a fantasy is experienced as compelling (and arguably the majority are not) it may find expression in real life, or in perverse scenarios. At the very least fantasy does represent a sexual reality, and gives expression to drives which do exist.

Accordingly, it becomes necessary to review the scarce literature on experienced feminine fantasy, as a prelude to examining its application, in sexual abuse and the associated abuse of self.

Friday, in her work "Women on Top", provides us with a rare insight into the vastly underrated and under researched phenomenon of female sexual fantasy.[6] While this is a work which may be vulnerable to academic criticism, it does provide for insights in this subject which are unavailable elsewhere in the literature. As Friday comments in her prologue,

> Here is a collective imagination that could not have existed 20 years ago, when women had no vocabulary, no permission, and no shared identity in which to describe their sexual feelings. Those first voices were tentative and filled with guilt, not for having done anything, but for simply daring to admit the inadvisable: that they had erotic thoughts which sexually aroused them. ....The assumption was that women did not have sexual fantasies.[7]

This, in common with other sets of assumptions, regarding the nature of female sexuality, will be challenged throughout the process of this paper.

In drawing upon a selected list of quotations from Friday's work, I am asserting the reality of both the erotic nature of 'feminine' thought or fantasy, and drawing attention to the dysjunction between this internal 'reality', and external social expectation, and socially constructed (or imposed) 'reality'. The greatest deficiency in our collective education is even in a rudimentary understanding of the true nature of feminine eroticism and sexuality. Not that this is the exclusive responsibility of men, most of whom are acutely unaware of any "gender conspiracy". Rather they too are the victims of libidinally dysfunctional socialisations as primarily regulated by women.

As Kaplan observes,

> However to this day the female voice is heard (or comprehended) as the call of the Siren, and whenever women speak up, men find new ways to denigrate and frighten them, to send them scurrying back to the shelters of motherhood and sexual purity. Women unaccustomed to commanding their own bodies and destinies, also tremble before the cryptic powers they discover within themselves. Even the women who dare to make themselves heard, then draw back because they are frightened of expressing the full range of their abilities and desires. Sometimes the bravest among them will subvert the causes they seem to be celebrating. [8]

In examining Friday's source material, 'Johana's' reported fantasy makes a direct association between maternalism, power, domination and sexuality.[9]

> I place one breast in his mouth, he sucks it for a few seconds and rejects it. I try the other one but the same thing happens. I get up squeeze my tits and find that my milk has dried up. I tell him to lie still and I go into the kitchen and squirt whipped cream on my nipples...He sucks and sucks on my nipples while I seductively rub my tits along his diapered penis. I begin to act stunned when I think it's enlarging. I open his diaper and find he is a man and tell him so. I ask him if he feels sore with pleasure and ready to burst. He nods yes. I take more jelly and rub it on him.[10]

As Friday comments in relation to "Linda's" fantasy,

> Is Linda's fantasy, so full of rage and sadistic revenge, a scenario of a man and woman? The punishments, the language, the anger itself, are rooted in the nursery. The fantasy sexualises the relationship of a naughty child and a mother. This time around, however, Linda is the powerful mother and the man stands where she once stood: dependent, begging, obedient, ultimately loving. She spanks him, scrubs him fiercely in the tub, gives him an enema, washes out his mouth with hot water, and convinces him in other 'loving' ways that from now on you're mine and mine alone.[11]

The most important observation here is the impulse toward role reversal, and identification with the aggressor, to a point where the dependent, passive, powerless little girl, becomes the powerful, dominant, sadistic woman.

Linda's fantasy continues.

> My fantasy has always been to dominate my partner. First off I call him up and tell him to drive over. He is to arrive in only a jockstrap, nothing more. And he is told to be there at a certain time. When he arrives he is five or ten minutes late. I push him forward over the back of a chair, so his face is pointing down toward the chair seat, and his rear is in the air. Pulling off my belt I give him fifteen hard smacks for being late.

Get down on your knees and ask for my forgiveness, I tell him, or you'll get fifteen more. He doesn't want any more so he obeys.[12]

Continuing the theme of the exercise of sadistic domination "Dawn" reports,

I chain him or tie his hands and tease, tease, tease, but he can't come until I decide, and I don't decide until he's miserable. Sometimes no sex at all, not really, I'm just slapping him, pulling his hair, and coming like crazy. Sometimes out of boredom and to hear him yell I shave his legs, always with soap, nobody should have that much pain. He objects and I move north, removing every hair and threatening more if he isn't perfectly still. I never castrate him, but he can never be sure...[13]

"Paloma's" reported fantasy continues the theme of sexual domination.

I like to be fucked in the ass, I like the incredible sensations, although we don't do this very often. Jeff doesn't like his rectum played with so... I fantasise he is being raped by a woman (me?) who has tied him up on the bed. She strips him, takes her clothes off and rubs her breasts on him (which he loves) and quickly he gets a hard on. She goes down on him and then, when he is screaming and happy, she pours oil all over his cock and ass and strokes his cock with one hand and puts her fingers up his ass with the other hand. He tries to squirm away but to no avail. He cries for mercy and she goes for his vibrator. She slowly inserts the vibrator (vibrating) into his asshole and then proceeds to mount his cock...[14]

A further reported fantasy also makes a manifest link between maternalism and eroticism.

I so badly want to possess this boy, sexually and maternally. To assert woman power by conquering him sexually, but also to maternally nurture him... I hold him in my arms like a baby, kissing him and stroking his beautiful hair.[15]

While the theme of maternalism and sexuality found expression in these fantasies, themes of control, domination, and aggression, commonly designated 'male' themes, were also evident in reported female fantasy. This would further suggest a commonality of sexual thought across gender lines, despite social proscription, and 'social' dichotomisation between what is male and what is female, particularly in relation to matters sexual.

He wants someone to dress him up like a woman, teach him how to be a good girl and basically dominate him during sex play. For some reason this gets me extremely hot... He moans softly and I tell him he better be quiet or else... Then I cover the fingers of my left hand well with the oil. I reach around him with my left hand and start moving my hand slowly up and down his shaft, while I press the outside of his anus with my right hand. Again I tell him that he is being a very good girl for his master and that it will all be over soon. I press my fingers further up his asshole and

26

speed up the rhythm of my other hand.... I have made myself come many times to this fantasy D and this is only the tip of the iceberg.[16]

Clearly this fantasy reveals a strong masculinity complex in the writer.

If need be they are punished. This is usually by making them drink a drink which has Spanish fly in it. The offender is then taken to a cold dark room and strapped to a wooden table so she cannot move. She is so overcome with lust and physical craving that she cannot control herself, and my pupils take turns taunting her.[17]

While this fantasy is sadistic and dominant, there is perhaps a discernible "identification with the aggressor".[18]

I take a couple of bites and my 'maid' just stands there with a huge erection waiting for my next command. Sometimes I command him to lie on the table and I eat my dinner off him.... sometimes I just tease him.[19]

Or sometimes they'll shove their cocks down my mouth, they know I can't do a thing about it. I mean, they know I would never fire them.[20]

In Friday's document themes of sexually sadistic domination and subjugation were highly evident.

In the following account the Freudian theme of "possession of the penis" is literally evident.

He is still trying not to get hard, but I will take care of that. I tell him to suck on my finger, telling him the wetter the better, as I am going to stick it up his ass. He gets it very wet. I quickly insert it up his ass and when I touch his gland he becomes instantly rock hard... I quickly tie a thin strip of leather around the base of his prick so I can keep him hard for as long as I want.[21]

The next vignette demonstrates the female's masculinity complex, penis envy, and the feminine sadistic impulse, in a highly graphic fashion.

I strap on a dildo and climb on top of her... I tease her for a while and then all of a sudden I poke it in. I then pull it out before she realises what has happened. She starts to cry. I hit her on the leg with the whip. I turn to see my boyfriend is thoroughly turned on. By the size of his erection, he looks like he is ready for his punishment.[22]

In this episode feminine aggressiveness and sadism is highly apparent.

In never never land I think of tortures and handcuffs and chains. I used to be aroused reading about torture, well I still am.[23]

The next quotation demonstrates the feminine desire for role-reversal, and the wish to assert a sadistic sexual primacy over the male.

> I found great sexual tension in dealing with this boy.... I'd show him what it was like being treated like a sex object... I made him pull down his jeans and lie across my lap in his shorts... I love spanking it... It's fantastic because I'm in control. I can do whatever I want.[24]

These insights into voluntarily submitted and unrestrained feminine fantasy carry a central importance for this text in that they convey, with disarming clarity, a reality of female sexuality, which directly contradicts societal expectations, and demands, of virtuosity. In normal circumstances, these themes remain secret and hidden, for very valid reasons. The themes identified here, 'maternal' sexual abuse, the exercise of sadistic sexual power, domination, control, punishment, and penetration, have a clear outlet for expression in the nursery. That is to say if society, and women themselves, are not prepared to accept and explore the parameters of their sexuality, these are likely to find expression in perverse scenarios. However, a first step on this path is increasing the collective knowledge of, and education about, the realities of experienced female sexuality. That is to say we must reverse the trend of requiring a separation between women and their sexuality, and begin a process of both understanding and accepting feminine sexuality. Under present circumstances the real perversion is structurally imposed, and rests with society and in its demands for conformity to a stereotype of femininity, which requires a separation between the true, sexual self, and a sexually passive, false self, conforming to the expectations of virtuous femininity. The latter being a sanitised, depersonalised and, at the extreme, dehumanised caricature, of the full potential of woman.

The very forces in society which deny and discount the parameters of sexuality experienced by women, are responsible for its frustrated enactment, whether manifesting in frigidity or neuroticism, mental illness or child abuse. Quite simply, if the libidinal impulse cannot find 'natural' or acceptable discharge, it may seek 'disguised' outlets, or expression, in perversion.

Notes

1   Freud, S. *New Introductory Lectures*, (Revision of Dream Theory), op. cit. p.27.
2   Ibid, (Joseph Popper-Lynkens), p. 222.
3   Ibid, p. 222.
4   Freud, S. *Totem and Taboo*, op. cit. p. 59.
5   Ibid, p. 59.
6   Friday, N. (1991) *Women on Top*, BCA, London.
7   Ibid, p. 6.
8   Kaplan, op. cit. p. 491.
9   Friday, op. cit. pp. 96/97.
10   Friday, op. cit. (Jonna's Story), pp. 96/97.
11   Friday, op. cit. (Linda), p. 138.

12   Friday, op. cit. (Jonna's Story), p. 138.
13   Friday, op. cit. (Dawn), p. 146.
14   Friday, op. cit. (Paloma), p. 144.
15   Friday, op. cit. (Theresa), p. 98.
16   Friday, op. cit . (Alison), p. 112.
17   Friday, op. cit . (Judith), p. 117.
18   Identification with aggressor.
19   Friday, op. cit. (Louellen), p. 122.
20   Friday, op. cit. (Louellen), p. 123.
21   Friday, op. cit. (Mandy), p. 141.
22   Friday, op. cit. (Kelly), p. 143.
23   Friday, op. cit. (Dawn), p. 145.
24   Friday, op. cit. (Ruth), p. 156.

4 Case histories: An analysis

My interest in this area of work - the parameters of female sexuality, and female child sexual abuse - developed primarily through my own clinical work. I have worked psychotherapeutically with some fifty patients over the past four years and of this number some six patients, or 12% of caseload, have disclosed material involving female sexual abuse of children. The point will be made in the text, that female abuse often involves a "masculine" dominant, sadistic tendency and this is deeply reflected in some of the case histories which follow. The evidence here and elsewhere in the text would suggest that the social notion of the feminine as the gentle sex, is primarily a social construct, formed to mask and defend against much darker and less acceptable psychical realities. The discussion of case histories which follow are very similar to other survivors accounts of abuse by females, to be considered later.

Patient C

Patient C was a lady in her thirties who had sexually abused her children, two boys and a girl. The abuse took place with all the children from the ages of 3-4 months. However, before considering her abusing behaviour, it is necessary to place this in the context of her own experience of abuse.

Patient C had been sexually abused by her father, and others, for as long as she could remember. She remembers being bathed as a young child in the front room by her mother, in front of the fire. Patient C deeply resented the fact that no regard was given to her privacy, and that others, including strangers, (to her) could watch her naked and vulnerable. This was to be a prelude to her own sexual abuse. Patient C's father was an extremely highly sexed man who "couldn't keep his hands off her". She would have been "fondled, prodded and poked" by her father on a weekly basis, and he would masturbate in front of her, while abusing her. By the age of 7 Patient C had been subjected to full sexual intercourse by her father which caused her great pain. She could remember bleeding, and trying (successfully) to hide this from her mother. Before long her father invited "family friends" to their home, to have sexual relations, and full intercourse with her. There was an abandoned car in the garden of the house where the sexual abuse, and sexual intercourse took place. Patient C subsequently came to regard the vehicle as the brothel. This lady's childhood history was completely dominated by the full parameters of sexual abuse by her father, and his numerous friends. A few examples will suffice in conveying the sexual realities of her childhood.

Patient C's father liked her to wear a school uniform and short skirts. Consequently she was required to wear a school uniform and short skirt even on occasion when she had to pick potatoes. She can remember being made to pick potatoes as a prelude to her abuse. At the age of approximately 10 she remembered standing (in her uniform) washing dishes at the kitchen sink. Her father came in, told her to bend over the sink, took her knickers off, and brutally buggered her. She could remember screaming as a result of the "searing pain". She was left lying on the floor by her father who "matter of factly" walked away. However Patient C did have ambivalent feelings about her sexual abuse. While in the main, she hated her abuse and being abused, sometimes she looked forward to her abuse, and enjoyed it. This was a dark secret for her, and was the source of enormous guilt, even when she was a child.

However the pathos of Patient C's childhood is perhaps best conveyed by recounting one of her "happy" memories. During late primary school Patient C had become attracted, and sexually attracted, to a boy in her class. She recalled a warm sunny summer day walking home with him, and she invited him into a grass field. They lay down together. and she stripped off her skirt and knickers, and allowed him to "feel her". She then pulled down his trousers and underwear, and attempted to have sex with him. She was aged approximately nine or ten. This was described as one of the happiest memories of childhood, and it was recalled by the patient in an innocent air of warmth and affection. (It had been a non-penetrative sexual encounter born out of affection rather than the painful sexual abuse she had come to perversely enjoy).

When aged 16 Patient C became pregnant to a soldier, and subsequently married him. Predictably perhaps he was a violent and abusive man. She purposefully became pregnant to escape from her home, and her sexually abusive father. However entrapped as she was in an external and internal world dominated by child sexual abuse she began abusing her own children from they were months old. This included playing with her young sons erections, masturbating them, penetrating their bottoms with fingers and objects. She would take them into the toilet and do "what ever she wanted with him". Patient C was totally without inhibition in satisfying the full parameters of her sexuality with her children. They were made to perform oral sex on her, and on each other. Her two sons were forced to penetrate her daughter. When they refused she would beat them on their naked bottoms "until they did". This recurrent theme of feminine sadistic dominant power was exemplified when she admitted to getting a kick of "seeing the fear in their wide eyes, their bodies trembling". "When I went for them they knew what was coming and they just wanted to sink into the ground ".... "but they were mine and I could do what ever I wanted with them". "I would just say right, come on you and I would take him into the toilet, masturbate him stick any finger up his bottom, make him penetrate me and have oral sex with me. If I wasn't satisfied I beat him, or her, or them, and made them do it again".

Patient C had been sexualised as a young child and was completely devoid of a socialised sexual morality. Her super-ego function in this regard was not even established, let alone underdeveloped. She had "learned" from her own childhood, that children existed to provide for adult sexual gratification, without qualification or question. Patient C's identity and her perceived value was, as a sexual object, and her obsessive pre-occupation was with sex. (Her experienced sexual abuse, her sexual attractedness to her children, their abuse, and her gratification). She was quite simply "acting out" the internalised view of self as assigned to her, as a pre-eminently sexual being, who's primary function was, as it had been, abusive sexual gratification. The patient sincerely expressed her conviction that she thought that that was normal and that it happened in all families. It was after all the reality of her childhood, and no-one had interceded on her behalf.

Patient A

Patient A was a 32 year old socially isolate male, who had abused a substantial number of children, males and females, from the ages of 10-14. He regarded himself as a "kind lover" who "never hurt" the children he abused. Patient A was a morose and socially isolate man, significantly located within the internal world where sexual fantasy involving young children dominated. He was a compulsive masturbator and derived what little comfort he could from this.

Patient A had spent his life in care, in various children's homes. One of these had been run by a religious order, and was staffed primarily by nuns. Patient A had been placed there, as a child from the age of 8 until he was 14, by which time he was regarded as "too disruptive" and was "moved on" to social services children's home. He was very well cared for in the later home and stated that the staff there "saved him". It was apparent that he retained a high regard for them.

Patient A informed me that he was "picked on" by the nuns from the age of ten (approximately) and punished. He informed me that this happened on a regular basis sometimes weekly. Patient A informed me that even when he had done nothing wrong, a reason would be fabricated to warrant his punishment. He was always punished by the Head of Home, who was a nun, and two other nuns. Patient A informed me that he would be taken to a room at the top of the house, where he was stripped naked and held down by two nuns. The Head of Home would then beat him with a curtain rail, across the bottom, legs and back. He remembered that he never cried, or screamed, "in front of them". Patient A was instructed "not to flinch his bottom", which was, of course involuntary, and this resulted in further punishment. The nuns would draw attention to "flinches of the bottom", claiming that he did it on purpose, demanding harder smacks that would "make his bottom flinch". Patient A recalled that the nuns got very "excited and giddy" during his punishment.

Usually on the day after a punishment the Head of Home would take Patient A out for a drive. She would pull his trousers down to inspect his bottom after the punishment. She always held his penis on these occasions. He started to get erections from the age of 11, and then she would masturbate him, and "play with it for ages". Significantly he was never allowed to touch her. Sometimes she would go shopping for underwear, and would ask him what colour of knickers he liked. On occasion she would make him wear the knickers while she masturbated him.

Patient A was enabled in making some connections with the rage and anger which were inevitably a consequence of his physical and sexual abuse. However he was heavily psychically defended against these emotions which were "acted out" in his own punishment, self imposed isolationism and in the replication of his own abuse, with other children His obsession with children's bottoms was similarly linked to the sexualisation and pre-occupation with his bottom by his abusers. The mixed messages of beatings, seduction, and sexualisation at the age of 1 1 had resulted in a fixation of sexual associations around that age. He clearly demonstrated a compulsion to repeat the circumstances of his own abuse with other children with the deeply sadistic component of that abuse, cloaked in his conviction of being a "kind lover" to the children he abused. His inability to form satisfactory relationships with adult women, socially or sexually was perhaps understandable. He found all adult women deeply threatening and developed instead occasional gay relationships with adult males.

Case B

Quite apart from the physical, and sadistic abuse Patient B endured during his childhood he went on to suffer sexual abuse by his sister, her friends, and an older woman.

Patient B had noticed that while his mother was beating him, to the point where he wet himself, his older sister would laugh. She would later make fun of him calling him a "wee girl". He felt that she had enjoyed observing his being abused by their mother.

On one occasion when the patient was aged 12, and alone in the house, he had assembled some girlie pictures on the floor of his bedroom. He had his trousers down masturbating to the photographs when his sister, then 15, and a girlfriend walked in. They called him a "dirty bastard", but told him not to stop. They then masturbated him in turn, to the point of ejaculation. However they didn't stop and took turns "playing" with him for about 30 minutes. They then said that they'd tell everybody in school what he had done, unless he did what they said. The next week they threatened to tell everyone unless he took of all his clothes and "masturbated" in front of them. They then both played with him laughing at his "wee dick".

Patient B was then instructed to "lick" both the girls through their knickers. They informed him to get on his knees to do this, and not to stop until he was told. When he refused his sister threatened to tell his father what he had done. Eventually the girls pulled off their knickers and Patient B had to "lick them" until, as he thought, they'd "peed in his mouth". After some months his sister

33

brought other friends home, and Patient B was made to masturbate in front of them and to give oral sex. They would laugh at him and generally treat him with derision. This went on for approximately a year when Patient B's sister became 16. After this Patient B continued to have oral sex with his sister, and began to have sexual intercourse with her. Sometimes they would be alone and sometimes a sister's girlfriend would be present. On occasion a girlfriend would just watch, or have oral sex performed on her, or full intercourse. Patient B had no say in the matter. It then transpired, when the patient was 13 an elder sister of one of the girlfriends had learned of what was going on. She arranged to meet patient B in a derelict house. "Philis" was an attractive adult woman in her mid twenties. When they first met Philis appeared very angry. She informed Patient B that she knew about what he was doing and she threatened to go to the police. Patient B pleaded with her not to but she appeared adamant. She then said that he needed to be punished, and asked if he had any ideas about what she could do. Patient B informed "Philis" that his father beat him with a strap. She enquired (and no doubt knew) was he stripped naked for these beatings. Patient B was then asked if he would prefer a "really good beating or the police to be informed". He elected for the beating, and was instructed to take all his clothes off (including his socks). "Philis" took off a thick leather belt from around her waist, and proceeded to beat Patient B around the bottom. The smacks were so hard Patient B moved a few steps upon each smack, so he was made to stand "with his backside out", with his hands on a wall. After a fairly severe beating lasting some ten minutes Philis sat down on an old box. She pulled up her skirt to reveal that she wasn't wearing knickers, and then instructed Patient B to "do it to her" (oral sex). He remembered that she was "absolutely soaking, more than the other girls". He began having full intercourse and oral sex with her, "almost every week-day until he was approximately fifteen and a half, and "she stopped it".

He met her some years after this and suggested re-establishing their sexual relationship however "she didn't want to know". "I was probably too old for her by that stage".

Case D

This was a male patient in his mid twenties, who suffered from a very high level of anxiety. His movements were very jerky and he suffered from severe hand trembling. He described his early childhood until the age of ten as reasonably happy, until he started "getting into trouble". His father began beating him with a belt almost on a weekly basis, and on one occasion beat him with a pole to such an extent that the pole broke over his back. However the worst physical abuse he suffered was at the hands of his mother, and it is contended here that this was sexually sadistic.

His mother would beat him with a belt, and with the buckle of the belt. He would be taken to his bedroom for his punishment, stripped naked and beaten, on his back, backside and legs. On more than one occasion he recalls receiving up to eight beatings in an afternoon. He would be beaten with the belt until welts and bruising appeared on his back, backside and legs. After about thirty minutes when "the stinging had started to go away" she would come in and beat him again, aiming the blows at the existing welts. He would scream and beg for mercy during these beatings but to no avail. During these occasions he described himself as being in a state of fear and terror. No matter how he tried to defend himself the lashes rained down. Patient D remembers wetting himself, and trying to protect himself by curling up "into a wee ball', but the beating continued. Sometimes Patient D was so badly beaten he could not attend school, and PE, because of the bruising to his legs. On other occasions when he did attend, he would have to stand in the classroom, as his bottom was too bruised and painful to sit. Patient D stated that his mother "did this for badness" and suggested that she enjoyed it. He would have been punished "at any time, for anything". Sometimes things would disappear in the house, i.e. a purse, for which he would be punished and beaten by his mother, after which, it would be miraculously found". While Patient D is not conscious of being sexually abused, he was aware that "she got something out of it". Patient D claimed that he could sense when he was to "get a beating". "It was like something came over her". Shortly after that he would be told, "right, your really going to get it this time. Get upstairs and get ready" (he had to take of his clothes and stand and wait for her). "Sometimes it was an hour before she came up". By the age of sixteen Patient D "couldn't take the abuse any more", and "had to get away from home". (By this time he was suffering more abuse by his father who by now was using his fists). Patient D was charged with the attempted murder and sexual assault of a young male child, but was not found guilty. This would have been fully consistent with the expression of a compulsion to repeat his own experience of sadistic brutal (sexual) assaults. It would have also provided a mechanism for the expression of the largely undischarged internal sense of rage and anger which continues to consume him. (This is currently expressed symptomatically in jerking movements, anxiety, trembling hands and speech, and in suicidal thoughts - turning the anger towards the self). In any event the alleged incident did serve to secure his "escape" from the family home and the abuse.

Patient E

Patient E was a professional female in her mid thirties who had been sexually abused as a child, between the ages of 11-14. This had involved mutual masturbation, but did not extend to penetration.

Patient E was extremely sexually attracted to young boys and would derive a sexual satisfaction from watching children play or by playing with children within her extended family. She had deeply sadistic sexual fantasies which involved children "being tied up" and beaten with "canes, straps, belts and whips" She commonly fantasised about doing this to me, as her therapist, and gave fantasised accounts of deeply sadistic sexual abuse. However the most significant fact with Patient E was the fact that she did not have children, because she knew "that she would sexually abuse them". The impulse to have children, "to abuse them" was in conflict with a super ego moral ascendancy, which resulted in her preference to be childless, rather than the sexual abuser of her own children.

Patient F

Patient F was a young man in his twenties who claimed to have been sexually abused by older girls, when he was aged between 10-13.

Patient F lived beside the coast, and he commonly played on a local beach. When aged ten he was approached by four older girls, aged approximately 14/15. They had surrounded him on one occasion and asked him to let them "see his willie". He remembered feeling slightly threatened and very embarrassed. One of the girls then unfastened his trousers and pulled them down to his ankles. The girls laughed at his "wee penis" and asked if he couldn't "get it up". Two of the girls "played" with his penis, and one performed oral sex upon him, but he failed to get an erection. They threatened to tell everyone that he couldn't get an erection, and went on to do precisely that Patient F remembered being taunted by the girls in his school to his great mortification. The same "gang" of girls continued to "get" him on the beach, and he would strip or they would strip him "for their amusement". When he was able to get erections they would take turns masturbating him, but he never enjoyed this and regarded it as sexual abuse. Patient F felt that this abuse by females served in determining his homosexual sexual orientation.

The themes identified in this case material, which points to a strongly sadistic sexual impulse in females, is entirely consistent with other survivors accounts to be considered later in this text.

5 Action research: Maternal and female sexual abuse

There are pervasive social, individual, inter-relational, psychical, and professional forces which contrive to make any realistic quantification of the extent of female, and maternal, sexual abuse, virtually impossible. Mothers are unlikely to seek help, as one consequence may be that their children are taken into care. (A case of one mother 'at risk' of sexually abusing children is considered, as is the professional response to her request for help). Females are unlikely to seek help as they may face prosecution. However, even if the motivation existed both mothers and females would have to face the credibility gap. They simply may not be believed. Professional resistance to "the problem" will be discussed, and this represents a serious educational and training deficiency in its own right.

Sons are unlikely to report abuse due to a variety of factors - credibility gap - likely impact on masculine persona - "perceived" uniqueness of abuse, reception into care - scapegoating and stigma - there may be a question of consensuality. (Interestingly, I have worked with both psychotherapy and social work students who were "sexually abused" by their mothers, and other females, as children, who claim that they enjoyed the experience, and were not harmed by it).

Daughters are unlikely to report for reasons approximating to the above, with the added consideration of their being perceived as lesbian. In the light of such factors mitigating against disclosure it becomes understandable that this secret problem has lacked in recognition, or indeed in any informed view as to its proportions.

The view was taken that of all professional groups, psychotherapists, would be the most likely group to encounter the phenomenon of specifically maternal sexual abuse, in professional practice. The "evidence" of abuse was considered equally valid, coming from an abuser, or victim.

A discrete region of the United Kingdom (which cannot be named for reasons of confidentiality) was selected, and forty very simple questionnaires were issued to 'registered' psychotherapists.

The research questionnaire attempted to ascertain the numbers of

1   Patients who were mothers.

2	Patients as mothers who disclosed an experienced sexual attraction toward their children (past and present).
3	Total Patient caseload
4	(i) Patients who had sexual contact with their mother.
	(ii) Patients who were sexually abused by their mother.

Of the forty questionnaires issued. twenty questionnaires were returned. For a variety of reasons, confidentiality, perceived lack of relevance, etc, seven of these were not comprehensibly completed, leaving a successful return ratio of 32.5%. Psychotherapy, and psychotherapeutic practice, is often viewed as being resistant to research penetration and subsequent analysis, principally to protect patient confidentiality. Psychotherapy also has a tradition of fragmentation, and rival schools within the totality of its community, i.e., in Great Britain, the Klienans, the Freudians and the Independents.

A similar dichotomy also exists within the research catchment area and it is being suggested here that one school may be disinclined to co-operate with the other for research purposes. Accordingly a 32.5 questionnaire return rate was actually quite good.

The second stage of the originally proposed research involved the formulation of a research instrument This was a carefully designed, and detailed 13 page questionnaire, which sought to examine in some detail in multifarious dimensions of maternal sexuality, maternal sexual contact, maternal sexual abuse, and its perceived consequences, within the context of psychotherapeutic interventions.

The approach was based upon the premise (informed by the review of literature and research as documented and professional experience) that maternal sexuality, and maternal sexual abuse was a commonly encountered phenomenon. The fact that this was not the case, posed a major difficulty, and the entire focus of the research has to be radically amended. The advantages of a comparatively macro approach were lost, so the relative strengths of micro, or action research approach had to be exploited. This involved trying to arrange for the selective interviewing of all those psychotherapists in the research area who had experience of this work. The detailed questionnaire approach was accordingly abandoned, and a semi-structured interview format adopted, simply and straightforwardly to ascertain.

The original research rationale

Mothers who have been sexually attracted to or who have had sexual contact with/abused their children

1	Number of patients in your caseload who have experienced sexual attraction toward their children.
2	How was disclosure made (i.e., was there resistance to uncovery)?
3	Did you anticipate the nature of the problem before disclosure?

4	What form of contact/abuse has taken place (if any)?
5	Has this resulted in psychical conflict and or neurotic symptoms in your patient?
6	Has this resulted in feelings of guilt?

Children sexually abused by mothers

I	Number of patients in your caseload who have disclosed sexual abuse by a mother.
2	How was this disclosure made, i.e. was there resistance to uncovery?
2A	What strategies did you use to counter resistance?
3	Did you anticipate the nature of the problem before disclosure?
4	Was the abuse consensual or enforced?
5	What form of contact or abuse has taken place?
6	Has this resulted in psychical conflict or neurotic symptoms?
7	Has this resulted in feelings of guilt?

The following action research, accordingly, has no pretension of being a scientifically informed work. It is accepted that any analysis or conclusions will have a casual inferential status. However even this provides us with knowledge base which was not previously available, and it does give rise to sets of questions which hopefully may result in further research. One conclusion is very clear, we need to develop a much greater body of knowledge in this subject area, and additionally this knowledge should inform our subsequent understanding and professional practice.

While accepting the limitations of this methodology, its validity should not be undermined. As Lawson (1993) observes "open ended interviews must be designed to obtain such depths of information and compensate for the brevity of survey questions".[1] In relation to the difficulties in examining maternal sexual abuse Trepper (1990) comments "the case study should not be considered non scientific, only non experimental. Science must incorporate both discovery and proof and the case study is an excellent method..."[2] Lawson (1993) goes on to make the extremely valid point, in relation to the problematic association between clinicians and researchers in this area.

Research on mother-son sexual abuse demands an exploratory, qualitative, or multi-method approach if social scientists are to reach a consensus regarding the prevalence of this phenomena.[3]

Presentation of findings

The first questionnaires issued will be analysed here in the following sequence.

| 1 | Presentation of data from all forms received. |

2   Breakdown of individual recorded incidence clustered into professional disciplines.

3   Breakdown of total recorded incidence upon the basis of allied professional background.

Observations

Presentation of interview material. Respondent and allied professional background.

    1   Psychotherapist/Psychiatrist
    2   Psychotherapist/Social Worker
    3   Psychotherapist/Nurse
    4   Psychotherapist/Psychiatrist.

Please note that all the statistical information relating to psychotherapists/psychiatrists extends to the totality of their patient caseload. They did not differentiate between patients who they saw as psychiatrists, and those who they saw as psychotherapists. This was not viewed as problematic in that the commonality is work with the mentally ill, the disturbed and the very disturbed. Arguably the more disturbed the patient is, the greater the likelihood that he or she has been abused.

As Freud observes,

> I therefore put forward the thesis that at the bottom of every case of hysteria there are one or more occurrences of premature sexual experiences, occurrences which belong to the earliest parts of childhood (Freud, 1896: 1962A, p203).

Psychiatrists therefore are as likely to encounter such pathologies in the course of their work, as psychotherapists in theirs, particularly given their demonstrated interest in psychotherapeutic approaches, and their professional training in that discipline.

The analysis of the data, and of additional findings, will be presented separately.

Interviews

Four of the six psychotherapists reporting experience in this area were interviewed. I was unable to arrange for an interview with one psychotherapist, despite repeated attempts. (She has reported two incidents of work with mothers sexually attracted to their children, two patients who had sexual contact with their mother. and two patients who had been sexually abused by their mother.) I did not arrange for an interview with one other psychotherapist who reported two incidents of patients who had "sexual contact" with their mothers, i.e., who were not abused. The inference being that this was a consensual contact. No other manifestation of "maternal perversion" was reported by this respondent and accordingly the view was taken that this was unexceptional.

Respondent 1 Psychotherapist/psychiatrist

		INCIDENCE RATIO
Approximated caseload	1000	
No of mothers as patients	200	
Experience of work with mothers sexually attracted to their children	0	0.200
No of patients who have (a) had sexual contact with their mother	1 or 2	1:1000 or 1:500
(b) who have been sexually abused by their mother	1 or 2	1:1000 or 1:500

Interviews

This respondent had indicated in his returned questionnaire

I recall one or two instances of inappropriate behaviour, but do not recall the details.

No further information was forthcoming, as details of the cases were difficult to recall. I felt that this was perfectly reasonable given the number of patients treated by the psychotherapist in question.

Respondent 2 Psychotherapist/Social Worker

		INCIDENCE RATIO
Approximated caseload	34	
No of mothers as patients	6	
Experience of work with mothers sexually attracted to their children	1	1:6
No of patients who have (a) had sexual contact with their mother	1	1:34
(b) who have been sexually abused by their mother	2	1:17

Interview - Case 1

Female, sexually abused by mother

The experience of abuse was disclosed in the early stages of my contact with this patient. There had been a history of social services involvement in relation to child care issues.

She relates her difficulties in caring for her own children, to her experience of being sexually abused. While she was abused by her mother she did not regard this with the same seriousness, as the abuse she had been exposed to by others. She experienced it in very different terms, compared to the sexual abuse she had suffered by men.

What form of sexual abuse did she experience with her mother?

There was a sort of sexual contact, an inappropriate genital stimulation. She felt that it was her mother's interventions with her genitalia which started her own interest in masturbation
She did not find this uncomfortable.

Was this sexual contact consensual?

My impression was that she did find it pleasurable. Her mother did not continue beyond a certain point, but she did herself.

Do you feel that this gave rise to conflict or guilt?

Probably not. There was a lot of inappropriate sexual behaviour in the family, extending to serious physical abuse by the mother.

Interview - Case 2

Mother sexually attracted to her children. 2F, 1M

Disclosure, in this case, was made with very great difficulty. She found herself very sexually interested in her son, however there was no sexual interest expressed in relation to her two daughters. She developed a sexual curiosity from bathing the boy, standing back and looking at him, she claimed to be fascinated by him sexually.
She really found it extremely difficult to talk about. She wanted to touch him, to fondle him, to play with his penis. This was experienced as a very strong impulse.
She was sexually attracted to him, almost beyond her control. She was enormously ashamed and frightened to talk about it.

Did you anticipate the nature of the problem in any way?

No, only in so far as her capacity to be a good mother was questioned by her. However I had previously encountered this, in that sense I was advantaged through previous experience. This experience of (maternal) child sexual abuse involved mother's continuing to sleep with their children, obsessive washing and bathing of children. Inappropriately continuing hygiene, one mother continuing to bath her 13 year old son.

Do you think this patient experienced conflict or guilt in relation to this sexual attractedness?

Yes, in an expressed form, there was an articulated difficulty and this was a source of considerable distress. However the distress was located in the awareness of the wish, it was not finding expression in symptoms.

I think that this incest desire is more commonly expressed in symptoms.

She really was very guilt ridden about the sexual attraction which she experienced toward her son. That was the central source of her not inconsiderable disturbance.

Interview - Case 3

Male, "abused" by his mother

There was very little resistance to uncovery about what may be termed sexual abuse by his mother, although he would not see this as abuse. The fact that he had been in therapy before no doubt helped in this regard. The disclosure (of maternal sexual abuse) was made relatively early, and was relatively straightforward.

Did you anticipate the nature of the problem?

No, however my general orientation would be one of aliveness to all possibilities, and I would tend to convey this through an empathetic and understanding disposition toward my patients.

Consensuality?

Yes, in my view the nature of his sexual involvement with his mother was consensual. There were two areas of (sexual) contact, during bathing and while sharing his mother's bed. He had a lot of contact with his depressed mother and he felt an obligation to support and be available to her in the absence of the father.

The sexual contact took the form of a touching of the genitals. She would comment upon his "being a big boy now, that's what happens!". He remembers the abuse aged about 4-5 until he was about 7, then there was a gap until he was aged from about 8 until he was 11. This would involve touching and fondling but did not extend to masturbation.

Were there feelings of guilt or conflict associated with this activity?

I do not think he felt guilty about it. More accurately one could say that he had feelings of ambivalence toward it. He has no distinct recollections of what precisely was happening during the early period (of abuse) other than the fact that he had a sexualised relationship with his mother. As far as he was concerned he was getting erections, through genital stimulation, and he found this pleasurable.

In oedipal terms he became the man. It was a reciprocal desire, a fulfilment of the oedipal wish.

Conflict?

Yes, there is an enormous and continuing conflict in terms of the current relationship with his mother and father. There is an enormous competitiveness within each of them (father and son). It continues to effect his relationships with other women. He deliberately chose as his wife someone who cannot meet his needs emotionally. Also, significantly, he chose a woman whose former husband was killed.

There is a continuing sexual dimension in his relationship with his mother.

Guilt?

Yes, but it is a guilt which gives rise to feelings which he can articulate. In this case the guilt has not been converted into symptoms.

Respondent 3   Psychotherapist

		INCIDENCE RATIO
Approximated caseload	40	
No of mothers as patients	12	
Experience of work with mothers sexually attracted to their children	2	1.6
No of patients who have had sexual contact with their mother	0	0.40
No of patients who have been sexually abused by their mother	1	1:40

Interview - Case 1

Young mother, 22, experiencing a strong sexual attraction toward her little boy

This was a fairly disturbed young lady who was resistant towards uncovery. It was very important to build a relationship of trust, acceptance and understanding with her. She was highly sensitive to any nuance of disapproval, even through tone or inflection. While the therapeutic stance has to be neutral, my responses to her would have been tinged with both empathy, and understanding. She had been badly (sexually) abused as a child, and was very disturbed as a consequence of this. She had an extremely low self esteem and self valuation. She was a self-cutter, which in itself is symptomatic of psychical conflict.

The sexual attraction she feels in relation to her little boy literally frightens her. She is constantly washing him, and clearly this is a source of arousal for her. The conflict here is in giving expression to her impulse to have sexual contact with her son, and the self disgust (proscription) she feels after doing it. Recently she has had to get a friend to bath him.

The child is on the at risk register for emotional abuse.

A lot of my work with her is around the validation of motherhood. To explain that it is normal to experience sexual feelings toward children, and that there is a sexual dimension in motherhood. However to also explain that there is a considerable distinction between experiencing such feelings, and acting upon them, or initiating contact.

Anticipation of problem?

No, but I don't as a rule discount any possibilities in human experience. I would tend to have an earthy approach, which is after all informed by Freudian theory.

Guilt?

Clearly she does suffer from acute guilt as a consequence of her sexual attraction for her little boy. She has no love for the girl children. Guilt is expressed as aggression. The boy is her love object.
She feels very guilty for having damaged or abused her little boy. She identifies the child with the men who have abused her!

Interview - Case 2

Adult male patient who was abused by his mother

The referring problem with this patient was that he wished to establish the reasons which lay behind his apparent inability to leave his wife. He presented with a host of guilt feelings around the prospect of leaving her. He had very pronounced, sadistic, sexual feelings toward his wife.

In this case the unconscious became conscious through transference.

His father had been imprisoned until he reached five years of age. They lived with an aunt and uncle in very cramped accommodation and he slept with his mother during these first five years of life. He remembers his mother coming up to the bedroom and repeatedly fondling his genitals, which held an excitement for him. At the time he associated both pleasure and fear with this sexual activity. A fear of the footsteps. There was a sense of guilt with it. There was a feeling of being angry with his father.

Anticipation of problem?

No I simply had not anticipated that that was at the source of the conflict and psychical disturbance. I would be much more inclined to look for that in the future.

There was a lot of psychical conflict, involving the mechanisms of denial and repression. In fact his wife was picking up on that a lot. Their relationship improved dramatically when he was enabled to locate the source of his anger, guilt, aggression and sadistic impulses.. His wife took the view that the therapeutic working through these issues saved their marriage.

Interview - Case 3

Female (mother, sexually attracted to her children)

This was from an assessment I was involved in undertaking but nevertheless it is within the context of my professional experience.

The lady had been sexually abused as a child, to the point where she probably could have been referred to as a sexualised child. She admitted that her children sexually excited her, however she did not admit to sexually abusing them. The view was taken that she was saying this for "shock value".

She said that she could no longer cream their bottoms, as she found this arousing. This activity reminded her of her own experience of abuse "which was quite exciting". She was trying to resist having thoughts of her own abuse.

She had been additionally physically and emotionally abused.

This particular case was not accepted for psychotherapy.

Respondent 4   Psychotherapist/Psychiatrist

		INCIDENCE RATIO
Approximated caseload	100	
No of mothers as patients	20	
Experience of work with mothers sexually attracted to their children	0	0.20
No of patients who have had sexual contact with their mother	0	0.0
No of patients who have been sexually abused by their mother	4	1:25

Case outlines

1   *Female* patient, who had extreme difficulty in discussing her experience of abuse.

    She had been residing in a hostel over a period of years and was referred to a sexual education group which would have involved disclosure and discussion of experienced abuse. She was so resistant to her enforced inclusion in the group that she left the hostel to return to the parental home.

    It was established that sexual abuse had taken place, and that this had involved her mother, but further details are not known. This patient was described as very disturbed, and clearly the experience was central to her condition.

2   *Female* patient. Contact with this patient was brief, and over a period of time.

Very few details were disclosed but the mother was actively involved in her sexual abuse, and co-abuse. Sexual abuse reportedly involved the whole family, and as a unit they were very resistant to disclosure and uncovery. This patient, now a mother herself, is "terrified of touching her children", because of her fear of abusing them. She apparently stated that she spends long periods of time in the bathroom with her children and there are strong suspicions that this may involve sexual contact and/or abuse, although this has not been disclosed.

3   *Male* patient (mentally handicapped). Disclosed having been sexually abused by his mother, but specific details are unknown. "His behaviour deteriorated when confronted with disclosure." Generally gets involved in very self-abusive behaviours.

4   *Female* patient. Attended 3 out of 10 arranged sessions at the psychosexual clinic.

Sexually abused by mother, details unknown. Presenting problem was a fear of marriage. It transpired that this patient was terrified of sex, which was directly linked to her fear of having babies, as she knew she would sexually abuse them. Child sexual abuse was a characteristic of the family culture, and was described as being an "intergenerational norm".

Upon approaching a previous psychiatrist with her problem, this patient was told "not to worry about it".

When I enquired from this psychotherapist/psychiatrist her views as to why such little detail of the abuse was known, she replied.

"Psychiatrists don't go down that road of sexuality and intimate relationships. If it's not on the history sheets it's avoided. Psychiatrists now are really dealing with major mental illness. Areas like this (sexual abuse, and the legacy of disturbance which derive from it) just don't get covered. There's an unspoken professional resistance towards it."

Interviewee	1	2	3	4
No of patients who are mothers	200	12	6	20
No of mothers who experienced sexual **A** attraction toward their children	0	2	1	0
TOTAL NO OF PATIENTS	1000	40	34	100
No of patients who have had sexual contact with mothers	1	0	1	0
No of patients who have been abused **B** by mother	1	1	2	4

INCIDENCE RATIO	A	0:200	1:6	1:6	0:20
Mothers sexually attracted to their children					

INCIDENCE RATIO	B	1:100	1:40	1:17	1:25

Patients reporting sexual contact with,
abuse by mother   0

Some of these reported incidence ratios, i.e. 1/6 were regarded as high. Particularly, bearing in mind that at the extreme this contrasts with reported incidence ratios of

A	0:450 }	mothers sexually attracted to their children
B	0:3000 }	patients sexually abused by their mothers

(Psychotherapist/Psychiatrist)

It would appear that a major variable is the openness of the professional worker, in exploring the existence and significance of female sexual abuse. Even more importantly perhaps may be an obvious professional ignorance, and a lack of empathic disposition, in facilitating such sensitive disclosure. This requires a human relations capability which clearly eludes perhaps a majority of professionals. Significantly the highest incident ratio was reported by a psychotherapist/nurse and the lowest by a psychotherapist/psychiatrist.

Notes

1   Lawson, C. (1993) *Mother-Son Sexual Abuse*: Rare or Under-reported Child Abuse and Neglect, 17: 261-269.
2   Trepper, T. A. (1990) In Celebration of the Case Study. *Journal of Family Psycho Therapy* 1(1) 5-13.
3   Lawson, op. cit. p. 268.

6 Analysis of findings

This breakdown of questionnaire replies establishes that all three professional groups have encountered the following.

1   Mothers who have expressed experiencing a sexual attraction toward their children, with five reported cases, out of a total of 2,125 mothers.
2   Patients who claim to have had sexual contact with their mothers, with six reported cases, out of a total of 7,339 patients.
3   Patients who have been sexually abused by their mothers, with ten reported cases out of a total of 7,339 patients.

Interestingly the replies of three respondents with a total caseload of 174 patients (of the 7,351 in total) accounted for 50% of work with patients who had been sexually abused by their mother, i.e., a ratio of 1:35, while the remaining psychotherapists reported an incidence of 1:1430.

Only six out of the thirteen respondents reported have any experience of these issues. Of these, five accounted for a caseload of 2,174 out of a total caseload of 7,351. That is to say it was relatively commonly encountered in their 2,174 caseload, but virtually not at all in the remaining 5,177 caseload of the majority of psychotherapists/psychiatrists/social workers et al.

Two respondents in particular reported professional experience with 4,500 general population patients, and 950 mothers as patients, had not encountered mothers who were sexually attracted toward their children, or patients of either sex who were either exposed to sexual contact, or sexual abuse with their mothers (both psychiatrists/ psychotherapists). This was qualified by one of these respondents "No young patients. Now working in general adult psychiatry". In contrast another respondent with experience of work with six mothers found one sexually attracted toward her children, and that in a general caseload of 35 that one had sexual contact with the mother, and that two had been sexually "abused" by the mother (social worker/psychotherapist).

Clearly such varied and disparate findings take us into the realms of phenomenology, and suggests that the significant variable is the knowledge, philosophical orientation, and interest level of the individual professional toward this problem. As documented previously it may well be a subject area which invokes great resistance, which may involve the internal world of the given, professional, through to moral, cultural, professional and sociological proscriptions to uncovery.

However if we insist upon not recognising this as a reality of the female experience, and not acknowledging the fact of female "perversion", we do ourselves a great disservice in terms of our understanding female sexuality. We are similarly disabled in working with "abused" children (as children or adults) and "abusing" mothers, where sensual and/or sexual contact is taken to this extreme.

To review Freud's observation of motherhood

> What we call affection will unfailingly show its effects on the genital zones as well.[1]

Weldon, of maternal incest,

> Nobody believes it is happening, sometimes even to the mother's chagrin.[2]

Weldon, of female sexual perversion

> We have all become silent conspirators in a system in which change could not be envisaged, since no-one would acknowledge that such behaviour existed ...[3]

> This failure has deprived some women of a better understanding of their difficulties.[4]

One could infer from this extremely limited research that a section of the psychotherapeutic community is beginning to uncover the reality of female sexual perversion in motherhood. That a majority is not, does not necessarily reflect on their professionalism. However it may be reflective of a personal, cultural and professional orientation, that really does not want to know, and indeed this is very understandable. Equally, it may be symptomatic of a rigid cultural and social proscription which actively mitigates against the disclosure of maternal or female perversion. Evidence is presented in this text which suggests that even when disclosure is made, it can be inappropriately responded to or ignored. This resulted in a report of one desperate patient attempting suicide such was her frustration at not being understood.

One conclusion of the statistics presented here would be that as a profession we all need to be more aware of the realities of female sexual "perversion", and more open to facilitating its disclosure.

As Freud (1898) observed,

> But an important consideration comes into play here - namely that a Doctor who is experienced in these things (concealed sexual life) does not meet his patients unprepared. and as a rule does not have to ask them for information but only for a confirmation of his surmises.[5]

Arguably this is a preferable philosophical and treatment disposition toward female and maternal perversion, than the incomprehension and disbelief which is all too commonly characteristic.

This would lend enormous weight to the observations of one psychotherapist/ psychiatrist interviewed when she commented,

> Psychiatrists don't go down that road of sexuality and intimate relationships. If it's not in the history sheets, it's avoided... Areas like this (sexual abuse, and the legacy of disturbance which derive from it) just don't get covered. There's an unspoken professional resistance towards it!

This resistance may be conscious, as this respondent suggests, or unconscious as suggested previously, but these statistics infer almost inescapably that such resistance exists. The analysis of the statistical data points to the prevalence of the problem, and strongly suggests proscription to uncovery, by patients, and professionals. The interview material graphically demonstrates the conflict and distress caused by this problem, both for mothers, and for the victims of sexual 'abuse'. Reid's research provided us with initial evidence.

To review the comments of his respondents,

> I was sure I had abused him, when it came to my mind I nearly went mad... I'm frightened to touch my children... I couldn't cope with the thought that I was sexually attracted to children.[6]

Another client reported,

> Yes I loved it. The more I abused her the more I needed to abuse.[7]

It was further reported,

> She had suffered a life time of tragedy and despair because of ill informed and misguided interventions from both professions.
> She was told it was no big deal and that quite a bit of it was in her imagination.
>
> She was told that she must have got something out of it.[8]

An analysis of the interview material advances these themes.

Respondent 2, Case 1

> She relates her difficulties in caring for her children, to her experience of being sexually abused (by her mother and others).

She felt that it was her mother's intervention with her genitalia which started her own interests in masturbation. Her mother did not continue beyond a certain point, but she did herself.

Respondent 2, Case 2

She found herself very sexually interested in her son...She found it extremely difficult to talk about...it was experienced as a very strong impulse....

She was sexually attracted to him, almost beyond her control....

She was very guilt ridden about the sexual attraction which she experienced toward her son, that was the central source of her not inconsiderable distress.

Respondent 2, Case 3 - Male patient sexually 'abused' by mother

Yes, in my view, the nature of his sexual involvement with his mother was consensual, during bathing and while sharing his mother's bed. The sexual contact took the form of a touching of the genitals. There is an enormous and continuing conflict in terms of the current relationships with his mother and father. He deliberately chose as his wife someone who cannot meet his needs emotionally. Also significantly he chose a women whose former husband was killed.

Respondent 3, Case 1 - Abusing mother

The sexual attraction she feels for her little boy literally frightens her. She is constantly washing him and clearly this is a source of arousal for her. Recently she has had to get a friend to bath him. She feels (acutely) guilty for having damaged or abused her little boy. The boy is her love object.

Respondent 3, Case 2 - Adult male patient sexually abused by his mother

He had very pronounced sadistic, sexual feelings toward his wife. He slept with his mother during the first five years of his life. He remembers his mother coming up to the bedroom and repeatedly fondling his genitals, which held excitement for him. At the time he associated both pleasure and fear with his sexual activity. There was a lot of psychical conflict.

Respondent 3, Case 3 - Sexually abusing mother?

She admitted that her children sexually excited her, however she did not admit to sexually abusing them. She said that she could no longer cream their bottoms as she found this arousing. The experience reminded her of her own experience of abuse which was quite exciting.

Respondent 4, Case 1 - Female patient abused by mother

It was established that sexual abuse had taken place and that this had involved her mother, but further details are not known.

Respondent 4, Case 2 - Female patient abused by mother

Very few details were disclosed but the mother was actually abused in her sexual abuse, and co-abuse. The patient, now a mother herself, is terrified of touching her children, because of her fear of abusing them.

Respondent 4, Case 3 - Male patient abused by mother

Disclosed having been sexually abused by mother. His behaviour deteriorates when confronted with this disclosure.

Respondent 4, Case 4 - Female patient abused by mother

Details unknown. Presenting problem, fear of marriage. It transpired that this patient was terrified of sex, which was directly limited to a fear of having babies, as she knew she would sexually abuse them.

On approaching a previous psychiatrist with her problem the patient was told not to worry about it (see Interviewee 4, Case 4).

This brief review of interview material advances us several important points.

1   The problem of maternal perversion does exist.
2   Some psychotherapists encounter the problem commonly, and particularly in the cases of respondents 2 and 3 (see main text) approach the problem in a highly informed sophisticated and skilled fashion.
3   By inference, that some professionals resist acknowledging the existence of the problem.
4   Some professionals respond to mothers seeking help with their "perverted" impulses in a very uninformed, insensitive and ignorant fashion. (If this is typical of professional responses towards uncovery, it is quite amazing that any mothers have felt confident enough to disclose "their special problem"[9] to any professional.)
5   That mothers who are sexually attracted toward their children are "guilt ridden, suffer considerable distress, experience extreme difficulty in touching their children, have fear of sex, can feel out of control, nearly go mad", [10] etc.
6   That children who have been abused by their mothers may experience a compulsion to repeat the abuse with their own children, that at the time the abuse may be consensual or pleasurable, that mothers sexual interventions may initiate masturbatory interest (as asserted by

Freud)[11] that the abuse may be central to conflict in current relationships, that it may determine the choice of partner, that sadistic, guilty and aggressive feelings associated with the abuse may be displaced onto present partner, etc. (See Interviewee 2, Case 3)

All the material thus far points to the existence of a "special problem" [12] (maternal "perversion") which has the potential to create enormous psychical distress for patients. The consequence for children abused by their mothers equally carries potential for conflict and distress which appears to impinge upon other significant relationships.

Professional understanding of, and treatment responses toward, this problem would appear to vary from denial (for whatever reasons) and rejection, to highly informed and empathetic approaches.

One theoretical link which appears to be neglected in the literature, which is very obvious, but simply rarely made is the fact that sexually abused children are significantly more likely to sexually abuse their children than "ordinary" parents. If vast majority of sexually abused children are female, the corrective implication is that women, as mothers, are more likely than men to become involved in sexually abusive activity.

Summary of findings

The following conclusions can be made from the presented material.

1   Maternal perversion does exist and it is commonly encountered by some psychotherapists.

2   Maternal perversion is quite likely to be much more prevalent than we realise, and this may be attributed to the fact that

A)   we are ignorant of its existence - quite simply we do not look for it, and consequently we do not encounter it.

B) we are unconsciously or consciously resistant to uncovery.

C)   it would also appear that some patients are well aware of our professional inadequacy in this regard, and that they have felt neither confident or facilitated in disclosure (accounts of gross mis-management have been documented)

3   We need to develop, as a matter of some priority, our knowledge of female sexuality and maternal perversion. Specialists in this field should be encouraged to share and impart their knowledge and experience. (This professional dialogue should extend to disinhibited and honest exchanges between male and female therapists, as has been the case during the process of this work.)

4   Female sexuality generally, and maternal perversion in particular, must be addressed much more rigorously in the education (and re-education where appropriate) and training of human relations professionals. This should extend to consider the consequences of maternal sexual abuse, both for children and adults.

5   More research into female and maternal perversion needs to be undertaken, that relevant professionals have a much more informed view, both of its nature and of its consequences.

As a society, we must be more instrumental in empowering women to recognise and discuss their experience of sexuality that they, and we, develop in understanding. To do otherwise, to carry on as before, is to tolerate the misunderstanding, the shame, the guilt and the distress, which many women tolerate alone.

Notes

1   Freud, S. (1975) *A Case of Hysteria, Three Essays on Sexuality and Other Works*, Vol VII, 1901-1905, Ed Strachey et al, Hogarth Press, London.
2   Weldon, C. V. (1988) *Mother Madonna Whore, The Idealisation and Denigration of Motherhood*, Free Association Books, London, p. 10.
3   Ibid, p. 5.
4   Ibid, p. 16.
5   Freud, S. (1975) *Sexual Aetiology of the Neurosis*, The Complete Works of Sigmund Freud, Strachey et al, Vol III, Early Psychoanalytic Publications, Hogarth Press, London, p. 266.
6   Reid, M. (1992) *Female Sexual Abuse*, Unpublished dissertation, Faculty of Social and Health Sciences, University of Ulster, p. 55.
7   Ibid, p. 61
8   Ibid, p. 63
9   Weldon, op. cit. p. 18.
10   Reid, op. cit. p. 55.
11   Freud, (1975) *New Introductory Lectures*, Ed Strachey, J. et al, Hogarth Press, London, p. 120.
12   Weldon, op. cit. p. 18.

7 The enactment of feminine perversion

Sexual perversion takes many forms, some of which may not be overtly sexual, as they may be shrouded in apparent respectability. Accordingly Victorians covering the legs of their grand pianos to avoid any sexual connotations, were in effect symbolising, in the drawing room, the very vulnerability to sexuality, their actions were designed to discount.[1] Similarly, draconian responses to infantile and childhood masturbation, through arousal and punishment, punishment, and genital mutilation, were acts of perversion providing for perverse sexual or psychical gratification.[2]

As documented, these perverse scenarios were extreme. To illustrate from one of the Freudian accounts previously quoted.

The young boy presented by his mother to the doctor to be punished for his masturbatory activity. Being made to take down his trousers and underpants, and to display the "offending organ", to his immense mortification. Being examined by the nurse who with some distaste holds the "offending organ" for the doctor's inspection. He shrieks of distress upon seeing the scissors to be used for the circumcision, his impending mutilation. His screams, heard by his mother, as the "jagged scissors" cut into the flesh of his penis. The immense pain as he limps home watched by a knowing public, to face the disapproval of his teachers, and the ridicule of his friends, and 'the girls'. Not only is he an outcast, he becomes the symbol of "the dirty", the unspeakable; sexuality. He represents that most terrible of all things, a sexually active child, a masturbator, a masturbator who will carry for all time the scars of his sexual punishment. His mother may tend the wound, inspect it regularly, to both prevent infection, but also to remind him of his "terrible crime".[3]

However this is not an act of morality, inspired by purity of thought, it is an act of base sexual sadism, cloaked in, of all things, social respectability. At a psychotherapeutic level there would be a number of explanatory approaches here.

1) This action may have been taken as a consequence of the mother's repressed sexual desire for her son, which refused to her in consciousness, found perverse expression in his sexual mutilation.

2) That her son, as an extension of her, was sexual was indicative of her own repressed sexuality, and vulnerability, which required further physical repression. That is in punishing her son she was purifying herself for her experienced sexuality, which 'had to be punished'.
3) That she resented her son's literally taking "possession of the penis".
4) That the mother's own repression of her sexuality had led to great psychical conflict in which her "unacceptable, masculine, sadistic", internal and unconscious impulses, found expression, in a socially acceptable way, i.e., in the sexual mutilation of her child and specifically of his penis.

Clearly these themes are not mutually exclusives or exhaustive, and the motivation to mutilate, may have been influenced by any combination of these psychical scenarios.

As Kaplan comments in relation to female perversion.

> In another female perversion womanliness itself is used as a masquerade that disguises the woman's forbidden masculine wishes... Similarly, nearly every female perversion disguises vengeful sadistic aims beneath a cloak of feminine masochism....

> a logical place to begin looking for a forbidden masculinity in females is beneath the nestling petticoats of a conventional female type.[4]

However while there is copious evidence attesting to feminine sadistic perversion, usually cloaked in the guise of respectability or morality, the feminine sadistic impulse may be more commonly turned toward the self,[5] that is to say perversely. (One view can be that sadistic impulses are vented on the self if they do not have alternative avenues of expression.)

The conflict in females between their innate, profound experienced sexuality, in the 'internal' world, and the internalised/socialised proscriptions and expectations, of the external world, are immense. Young girls in particular can be placed in a position of apparently irresolvable contradiction between the internal sexual reality of self, and the expectations of the external[5] social audience, who implicitly and explicitly demand conformity to a feminine 'ideal type'.

The social imperative of female purity and virtuosity, becomes internalised through super-ego function, interceding at times viciously, against sexual transgression, or even thought. This is central to the matrix of conflict into which young girls are placed, the conflict between id dominated libidinal impulses and drives, and super-ego responses dedicated to their suppression and denial. While we can understand and comprehend these forces, in the context of their social and internal pathology, the force, and commonly the effect of anti-libidinal tendency within both girls and women would suggest an even deeper and more primal factor. The Jungian concept of the collective unconscious would appear to have a possible relevance here.[6, 7] That the libidinal impulse toward sexuality is countered by an antilibidinal impulse, experienced internally and collectively, regulated through the society of women acting out their inheritance of disallowed sexuality and "endogenous" guilt. This finds expression in repression and perversion, in the punishment of sexuality internally, within themselves, and in other women, and maternally with their children, most of all, with their female children. [8]

While the castration complex in boys results in fear, a fear of losing the penis at the hands of a jealous father, the castration complex in girls would appear as viable a threat, both in history, and in the treatment of women in contemporary society.[9] However while the castration complex in boys involves fear, and by association, passivity, the actual (perceived) castration of the female must involve rage, and by implication, aggressiveness. Bear in mind that this comes as the third psychical trauma borne by females, which does not similarly effect their male counterparts, i.e., the necessary transfer of affection and erotic desire from the original love object, the mother, 'displaced' on to the father; the original 'assault' on female sexuality, the fact that she is dispossessed of a penis, giving rise to penis envy,[10] and finally the fact that her self, her sexual self, is disallowed and unaccepted.

It would be difficult to envisage that such a loss of 'sexual love', sense of sexual inferiority, and discountment of the true self, would be met by any response other than 'ego anger' and aggression. However even this has to be subordinated and repressed under super-ego ascendancy. This clearly involves the potential for massive psychical conflict, in what are "normal" and "ordinary" circumstances, for the female. In reality however this is an extraordinary contrivance of circumstance, which can be difficult to intellectually comprehend in its import; the affective consequences of which we are inferring. The aggression which must be experienced by the female, albeit not allowed into consciousness, is repressed for valid reasons, its full comprehension may be overwhelming, given the impossibility of its resolution. Accordingly the last of these three traumatic events, the discovery of the inferior sexual self must be defended against, and compensated for. As a consequence the feminine experience of sexuality may be "split off", repressed, denied, buried under the dominance of super-ego function. However the sexual impulses and drives emanating from the id (which are commonly sadistic and sexually punitive) demand "outlet" or "discharge" may find expression in dreams, fantasy, or perverse scenarios which gives expression to the otherwise forbidden aggressive femininity. Alternatively the feminine denial of the sexual self may necessitate its expression symptomatically finding an outlet in sexual punishment (becoming asexual to atone for experienced sexuality), through becoming isolate, unrelational, neurotic, depressed, histrionic, paranoid, awkward and blushing in male company, obese, bulimic, anorexic, mad. That is in circumstances where female libidinal aggressiveness is turned toward the self.

A further factor contributing to a disposition of relative neuroticism, and perceptions of gender disadvantage in women, may be identified in the fact that the birth of a female child, may be seen as, at times, a poor second best, to a male child. This is a phenomenon commonly encountered in clinical practice and it can often be central to psychical "disturbance", identity and sexual identity, crisis. While the perception of inferiority may not find expression or articulation with young girls and their parents, its reality can find subliminal expression through being "acted out" by female children in a "tomboy" phase of development. Significantly however its real import is centrally located in sexual difference, with its associative connotations for identity and specifically sexual identity, and acceptance (both in terms of the constellation of external relationships, and ultimately of the self). Perceptions of differential acceptance and even partial rejection may be internalised and converted into a non-acceptance of self, and a rejection of the sexual self - (a theme with direct implications for the anorexic patient).

The oppressive realities which surround the female child creates psychical conflict and trauma which almost of necessity must give rise to aggression and an associated symptomatic consequence. This process of mediation for the female and the feminine, between those dichotomised and polarised extremes, the "good", moral, virtuous, pure, girl, and the bad sexual girl, creates the circumstances for an almost developmentally required psychical struggle. To be "good" is to abandon the true sexual self, to be "bad" is to risk rejection from the matrix of human relationships, family, friends and peers, crucial to identity.

All of this lends itself to analysis within the existentialists's conceptual framework.[11,12,13,14] That for females, all social systems, structures, institutions, networks, all informal and formal human organisations, in particular the family, results in conspiracy. A conspiracy which carries an enviable consequence of the alienation of the female from herself, and the loss of true identity and sexual aggressiveness, which must be sacrificed to meet the demands and the expectations of the external audience. It represents a manifestation of the social construction of reality, in extremis, often at great cost to the females true, or virtual, self, that is the "necessary" negation of the erotic self. While the family is central to the oppression of this scenario, it is the maternal system in particular, which conspires to discount and negate the erotic dimension of the female child and the woman. Just as the circumcised and desexualised women of the third world may be the strongest advocates of female morality and female circumcision, mothers in the West may achieve their equally sadistic sexual aims, against their daughters, psychically. The consequence bears a remarkable similarity. The extent of the psychical trauma posed through the awakening or reawakening of sexuality in females at puberty, against the demands for purity and virtuosity, regulated internally through the super-ego, and externally through social expectation, may manifest in the condition of anorexia.

Anorexia nervosa (as a specific and discrete condition) is virtually unknown in females before the age of puberty, usually around eleven. When the girl becomes sexually active she encounters the kinds of psychical and sexual conflicts as previously outlined in this chapter. The clean, pure, virtuous little girl is suddenly confronted with her "dirty" sexuality and genital strivings. In the mind of the anorexic this becomes a struggle between good and bad. The good little girl, assisted by a super-ego unforgiving of any, except saintly behaviour, and her mother, similarly sexually repressed given her conformity to the demands of the external world, conspire to resist the impulses and drives of emergent sexuality.

Usually the perfect little girl, conforming to all the wishes and aspirations of the mother, forms an attachment with her, the asexual madonna, which becomes incorporated within the child's "parental agency"; the superego. The more developed this bond, the more affectively dependent the girl is upon her mother, the more difficult the separation/individuation process becomes. To some extent it represents a form of "identification with the aggressor", an aggressor whose intent is the suppression of the girls true, sexual self, and whose aims have been psychically incorporated in infancy, and retained within the "timelessness" of the id.[15]

The libidinal impulse is accordingly denied expression in sexuality, and seeks alternative discharge through the punishment and mortification of the self. She starves herself of the food that would transform her body from gender ambiguous, to that of a sexually mature woman. She is the embodiment of virtue, which is by definition (for her) asexual, any thoughts of sex and genitals or masturbation, is responded to by punishment, the mortification of the flesh, through starvation. Accordingly the girl gives perverse expression to the libidinal impulse and in so doing through self punishment acquires power over her once powerful parents. In her perversion she can humiliate and defeat them through means of her emaciation. She finds a power in her sexual punishment, beyond that which she could realise through her sexuality. As previously discussed interventions, in this case medical and psychiatric, only serve to amplify and stimulate the problem they seek to resolve. It almost serves as a case in point that the medical profession seem incapable of comprehending the relationship between sexuality and mental functioning, and certainly to understanding anorexia nervosa as the expression of sexuality, as a sexual perversion.

As Kaplan comments,

> While the doctors were figuring out how to classify and label this disorder, it got around that some 15% of anorectics died of starvation, and this fact, because it increased the anxieties of anorectics' families and their doctors, contributed to the blurring of everyone's vision about the underlying meaning of the refusal to eat and compulsive emaciation.
>
> When someone you love or care for is dying right before your eyes, you don't bother to worry about underlying meanings. When someone is starving to death, you force feed her by mouth or by nasogastric tubes, you give her insulin therapy designed to bring on sweating, dizziness, anxiety and eventually hunger; you coax her to swallow chlorpromazine to reduce her fear of eating; you anaesthetise her so that you can perform neurosurgery on her brain, the leucotomy that gets her to eat but turns her into a bulimic, a secret binger-vomiter. In short, medical responses which maximise the girls humiliation and punishment. Through all this the anorectic is unconsciously victorious, for her these mortifications of her flesh are a collaboration with her unconscious perverse scenario".[16]

Anorexia nervosa therefore becomes the perverse sado-masochistic expression of a forbidden masculine sexuality, it does not involve beating, whipping, humiliating, mutilating, stimulating and depriving, chaining or strapping of sexual objects on the self as previously documented; in this instance it involves the expression of sexuality through starvation, which can ultimately result in death. The victory of thantos over libido, or perversely the evocation of death, as the protector of purity, against the sexual. The good little girl, who died rather than accept the true, sexual self. (However the real debate lies in the location of blame. With the girl, in her expression of sexual perversion, or the mother and her imperative of the denial of sexuality, and the family and societal expectation of virtue and purity, requiring the denial of the sexual self, and the associated psychical conflict, which can be 'acted out' to the point of death).

In some cases a connection can be made between the sexual basis of the conflict, which manifests in anorexia, and its perverse expression in punitive eroticism, which may result in an outlet for the psychical conflict, and its resolution.

> One woman who eventually recovered recalled the very moment she had arrived at perfection. The force feedings and the chlorpromazine had failed to cure her and even encouraged her rebellion and heightened her erotic longings. She was on the brink of death. She didn't care anymore what her parents or her doctors thought about the state of her mind or the appearance of her body. She needed only her own mirror to reflect back the perfection she had been striving for and finally achieved. 'I got my wish to be a third sex, both girl and boy. Standing in front of the mirror, I saw a lovely attractive woman. My other self, the body outside the mirror, was a lusting young man preparing to seduce the girl in the mirror. I was having a love affair with myself'. [17]

This provides a fascinating example of the resolution of psychical conflict, at a point of near death. The three psychically conflicting elements came together in an experienced erotic fusion, a connectedness negating the psychical struggle, caused formerly by their mutual opposition. The girl's sexual self, represented erotically, her internalised super ego dominated asexual self, and her forbidden masculine self, culminating in a "love affair", or more accurately a discovery and acceptance of the true self, as sexual.

The erotic life, or inner world of women, as evidenced in their accounts of sexual fantasy (Chapter III) clearly has an avenue of expression, perversely, in the maternal role. It provides for the ideal cover, the perfect disguise, the pure, virtuous, revered status of the loving mother, may mask a darker reality, the sexual, sadistic, cruel and abusive mother.

Many of the accounts of female erotic fantasy made a direct connection between maternalism and sexuality, in which total power, domination, and sexual sadism featured prominently. As in this not unrepresentative account, from Friday's source material.

> Another of my favourite activities in infantilism (as the "mommy")..... I am genuinely (sexually) turned on by it, too, it's a unique combination of mother baby cosiness and total domination. [18]

In this fantasy account it is apparent that the maternal role can be used as a means of expressing 'masculine' sexuality, in the form of sexual domination.

Another account, in fantasy, carries a clear application for female, maternal, child sexual abuse.

After our first night of sex I am still kind to him but less gentle. I teach him how to hold his ejaculation until I want him to release it, and occasionally I have to paddle his boney ass to get him to try harder. He becomes very good at it as well as sucking my breasts and clit exactly how I've taught him to... He knows I would never harm him, but sometimes he disobeys and he gets his little butt paddled, hard... I also like to stick my finger up his ass or squeeze his buttocks together as we're coming. Other times I slide a vibrator up him and keep it there as I screw him mercilessly. At first the size of it scares him and he's tight as he pleads with me not to force it in. But I tie his wrists to the bedposts and push his knees up to his chest and slowly inch it in, always well lubricated. He is very noisy when I do anything sexual to him.[19]

I include the female erotic fantasy accounts to explore the following proposition - That if women have highly erotic fantasies (and the evidence presented here suggests that they do), and if this allows for the expression of "masculine" sexuality normally forbidden to them, are precisely these impulses and drives likely to find expression, given, opportunity. That is to say, that if, the experienced erotic "masculine" impulses and drives cannot find expression in adult or marital sexual relationships, is it possible that they may find expression perversely, with children.
As Friday comments,

I have saved my comment on Gabby's fantasy of initiating her son into sex because she is the only mother in my research to admit to the idea, though I imagine it is commonplace, but quickly repressed.[20]

However there is little evidence of repression in the accounts of female erotic fantasy, as presented by Friday. We have instead inferences and allusions to maternal sexuality, we even have accounts of women's sexual relations with animals, but not with their sons and daughters, where the opportunities for enactment abound. As with most female perversion, the anorexic, the moralist, and the mad, the true nature of the female sexual conflict is commonly disguised or deflected.
Thus while we have copious accounts of sexual, or sexualised, power, domination, control, sadism, penetration, punishment, masturbation, oral sex, spanking, bondage, only one female respondent 'overtly' reported a sexual relationship with her child. Such a studied need for the "repression" of this desire, even in fantasy, provides evidence of its existence in reality.
Indeed Friday goes on to apparently, if ambiguously, make this point.

Perhaps mothers' incest fantasies are seldom heard as explanation for their stepping back emotionally and physically from their sons because mother doesn't step back, withdraw, not ever.[21]

A boy cannot tell his mother where to draw the line - a part of him doesn't want her to - nor does society scold her for acts a father would be jailed for committing with his daughters.[22]

This is a very significant statement and one worthy of reflection. It suggests a social collusiveness with what could readily be regarded as maternal sexual abuse of sons, and it also implies a normality of this form of female "perversion". (Although Fisher's research, (1990) did suggest that males sexually abused by females when they were children enjoyed the experience.)

However our purpose is now to consider the inter-relationship between female erotic fantasies, opportunity, and forms of female initiated child sexual abuse.

The realities of child sexual abuse, predictably, approximate to the sexual themes reported in accounts of female erotic fantasy. Sexual domination, sexual punishment and sexual control, as evidenced in Elliot's research, reporting the experiences of an abused male.

> ....During the 1940's I was sent to a boarding school for children without fathers. The residential staff were all unmarried ladies who seemed to enjoy delivering frequent punishments in front of an audience. For example, if boys misbehaved during a meal, they were taken across to the girls' table, had their trousers taken down, and were spanked in front of the girls. Or we would be taken to the Matron's bedroom while she was in bed, and had our bare bottoms smacked while she and several others watched. The sexual dimension was always there. There was much talk of bottoms, spankings, and who was doing what to whom.[23]

Another of Elliots male respondents was simply disbelieved by his therapist when trying to convey his experience of sexual abuse, by his mother.

> I tried to tell my therapist when I was 35. She told me that I was having fantasies about my mother and that I needed more therapy to deal with it.

> ...In reality my mother had sexually abused me for as long as I could remember. The abuse was horrific, including beatings and sado-masochistic sex.[24]

Sgroi and Sargent report from their review of case histories.

> In this case the abuse by the mother (of her son) included bondage, mutual sexual fondling, reciprocal oral sex, reciprocal administration of enemas and sexual penetration with other objects.

> The mother involved carried out the same practices with her daughter... In 'case 8', a female reported "sexual abuse by the mother included bondage, genital fondling, oral sex, penetration with objects, being subjected to sexual contact with animals, to witnessing sexual interactions between her parents". Another female victim of maternal sexual abuse reported receiving enemas on a daily basis, from the age of 4, until 18.[25]

Similarly Hunter reports of 'Lucy', a client undergoing counselling for her abuse.

...Lucy told me that she had been sexually abused by her mother from the age of two. ....The sexual abuse continued until Lucy was twelve. It involved vaginal penetration with sharp objects, being forced to sexually stimulate her mother and on occasion being abused by a boyfriend of her mothers.... She would then produce various items to insert into my vagina or anus. Sometimes she used only her fingers. [26]

However, it is from the literature of the survivors that we get the greatest insight into the potential perverseness of female sexuality. While the sadomasochistic themes identified in erotic feminine fantasy rarely found expression with their most likely target, children, at a reported level, however what we encounter in reality is entirely different.

Female survivors stories

In *Eleanor's story* we find

At first the abuse was mild. She used to lie me on the bed, take off my nappy and gently stroke between my legs ...

One fateful day she took me to the bathroom with her. I was to play on the floor with my toys while she had a bath. When she got out she put the lid of the toilet down and sat on it. Bracing one leg on the bath and the other on the side of the airing cupboard she drew me to her. She took my hands and guided them toward her genitals... She persisted and slowly with my tiny child's hands I tried to do as she wanted. Her breathing grew heavy and faster and eventually she threw back her head and let out a large scream. [27]

In *Lynne's story* we encounter maternal sexuality, sexual punishment, and the enactment of perverse scenarios, more extreme than any of the fantasy accounts. [28]

The initial memories of abuse were that of being fondled which probably began in infancy. By the time I was three years old, mother was having me touch her as well. Later I was introduced to oral sex. This sort of behaviour continued almost nightly until I was twelve years of age. This in itself was horrible enough, but by the time I entered school Mother started torturing me in sexual ways.

The first time I remember being sexually tortured was when mother took me to a wooded area, fondled me, had oral sex with me, and inserted her fingers into my vagina. I cried and screamed because of the pain. This only made mother angry, so to shut me up and to threaten me she picked up a large stick and shoved it inside my vagina. This incident taught me a lesson of silence and to turn off feelings of pain.

At the age of five I wanted some attention from mother; but she was too busy ironing. I accidentally knocked off the old sprinkling bottle and broke it. Mother was furious. She dragged me off to the bedroom and chained me, spread-eagled, to the bed. Then she took a piece of the broken glass and lacerated the inside of my vagina with it. [29]

In addition, Lynne, as a child, had to endure further 'sexual torture' at her mother's hands, including; "having the edges of the vaginal opening cut with scissors, being sexually penetrated with pencils, wooden spoons, coat hangers, and even lit cigarettes". [30]

"Karen" gives her account of maternal abuse. [31]

I was sexually abused by my mother from the age of one until I was ten years old. When I was thirteen, she forcibly broke my hymen so that my father and brother could rape me. [32]

In an interesting development of her story, Karen goes on to make comments which have a clear application to the concept of inter-generational maternal abuse, i.e., maternal abuse as a "learned" or "culturally transmitted" behaviour. This sociological approach has as its psychotherapeutic equivalent the notion of a "compulsion to repeat", in this case, personally experienced abuse, with one's own children.

It took another two years before I had a dream that I was sexually abusing my own daughter - to my horror. [33]

While fully accepting the sentiment, the Freudian view obtains that in every dream there is a concealed wish - in this case not heavily concealed - and accordingly the horror is a compensatory defensive posture, defending against the sexual, maternal desire.

Karen goes on to state significantly

I told my sister, who I found out was also a victim of the abuse from my mother, father and brother. I think looking back that my mother was abused by her mother. She occasionally made comments about it, although she said that it was done in the name of love. My mother then told me that this is what her mother did to her and that when I had a daughter I would understand. When I talked to my sister, I suspected that she had gone on to sexually abuse her own children, now grown up. [34]

"Gillian's story" also suggests the compulsion to repeat, or "repetition compulsion theme". [35]

I know from some of the things she has told me that she herself was probably abused as a child, and I am certain that the events I have recalled, with the help of a therapist, are completely buried in her mind. She even told me once that she has a place right down at the back of her memory where she pushes the unhappy times. [36]

After Gillian had been beaten by her father with a belt for slapping her sister, and forced to "suck his penis", he left the room and her mother returned. [37]

My mother came back with the baby. She then turned to me as I lay limp and without knickers on the bed.

She took the hairbrush from the dressing table and rammed its handle into my vagina - I have a lasting memory of the fury on her face. The pain was enormous. Then she stopped that and instead began to fondle me, using her finger to bring me to a climax. I had an orgasm which overwhelmed me and then she seemed angry again, slamming the hairbrush handle back into me and saying, 'Don't you ever do that again'....

"I realise, too, that she was beside herself with anger and fear for the baby, and this must have caused her to repeat a forgotten pattern of her own childhood.[39]

Rachael's story [40]

I had been sexually abused by my mother, in various ways, from the age of two until the age of nine...

She wanted more - she wanted me to enjoy it, even to ask for it. She wanted to be kissed on the lips, courted and admired. She wanted me to be the perfect lover. She taught me to sit astride her, froglike, and bounce up and down.... If I didn't wash up properly, or bring her coffee in bed in the morning, she would spank me, kiss my bottom better, then she would turn me over and stroke my budding genitals, saying what a naughty girl I was, and how lucky she loved me.[41]

In *Sarah's story* we find an articulation of the sense of betrayal which permeates female victims accounts of maternal abuse.[42]

You spanked a hurt and defenceless little girl for being so abused that she was in constant pain and fear. That was abuse, mother. You showed me no compassion, no understanding, no decency. That was abuse.[43]

In both fantasies, and in the victims accounts of abuse we have clear evidence of the female erotic wish to "penetrate" anally, vaginally, orally, to "penetrate" the skin by beating, smacking, caning, whipping, to "penetrate" the stomach through the administration of enemas, etc. In the male victims account of sexual abuse by mothers, and females, which follows, the "penetrative beating" is much more pronounced, which appears to symbolically represent vaginal penetration with the penis. As Faller suggests, female abusers appear much more preoccupied with penetrative and sadistic sex than their male counterparts.[44] This is actually extremely significant. As discussed previously the developmental traumas with which girls, unlike boys have to contend - change of love object, penis envy, non-acceptance of their true sexuality - must evoke an ego response of anger, resentment, disillusionment, and alienation from the true (sexual) self. In turn this must inevitably result in a state of psychical conflict which may find expression symptomatically, neurosis, hysteria, obsession/compulsive behaviours, anorexia, or more commonly in a splitting between the true, and the socially presented self. In most of these responses we can detect a responsive sadistic impulse directed toward the self with consequences ranging from mildly dysfunctional, to life threatening. The reactive 'masculine' sadistic impulse is managed in such a way because, usually, it has no alternative means of expression, or discharge. That is not to say that these sadistic impulses are not seeking alternative expression, as in both the accounts of female erotic fantasy (the wish), and abuse (the enactment), they are psychically, and actually discharged. The fingers, pencils, sticks, hands, coat hangers, canes, whips, hairbrush handles, etc, are psychically and symbolically the avenging, abusive penis, used to dominate and control, to "penetrate" and tear with "rhythmic" regularity. These penetrative objects represent the penis, used aggressively and in frustration, emanating from the female masculinity complex. As documented previously, mothers and females administering enemas can be both sexual, and sadistically abusive. This classically embodies the female masculinity complex in both the exercise of aggressive sexual power, and penetration. This is an almost uniquely female perversion, with no accounts in the literature, that we have encountered, of male involvement. Quintano was so concerned both about the prevalence, and consequences of abusive enema usage, that he recommended clinicians to enquire about this in initial patient assessment.

> From these evaluations I've discovered a number of patients who recall the early experience of enema as having been forceful, aggressive, intrusive and in violation of think boundaries.[45]

The sadistic impulse is born from the females sense of castration, her genital inferiority, and her "shame". It is no coincidence that femininity presents as so oppositional to the female's sadistic sexual reality, which it is essentially evolved to conceal, most of all to the woman herself. As Morris, in 'The Naked Ape', points out,

> The rhythmic pelvic thrusts have become symbolically modified to the rhythmic blows of the cane.[46] (Or the other penetrative devices, as documented).

And this may have a complementality with the sexual and erotic psychology of men, many of whom secretly wish to give expression to the passive, submissive feminine self. As the female strives to give expression to her secret and forbidden masculinity, men may seek to express the feminine self. But such feelings are forbidden, and consequently must be buried and usually are repressed from consciousness.

Freud (1919) in 'A Child Being Beaten' believed that "the boy's beating fantasy is...passive from the very beginning, and is derived from a feminine attitude toward his father" (XVII p. 198).[47]

As Rousseau comments with regard to his "flagellant obsession" (in Jean Jacques Rousseau's 'Confessions', 1782)

> Who would have supposed that this childish punishment received at the age of eight at the hands of a woman of thirty, would determine my tastes and desires, my passions, my very self for the rest of my life, and that in a sense diametrically opposed to the one in which they should have

developed? At the moment when my senses were aroused my desires took a false turn and, confining themselves to this early experience, never set about seeking a different one. With sensuality burning in my blood almost from my birth, I kept myself pure and unsullied up to an age when even the coldest and most backward natures have developed. Tormented for a long while by I knew not what, I feasted my eyes on lovely women, recalling them ceaselessly to my imagination, but only to make use of them in my own fashion as so many Mlle Lamberciers.[48] (The latter being the woman who had subjected him to 'childish punishment'.)

This brings to mind a case discussed at a psychotherapy training seminar, involving a patient with a "PVC" and spanking fetish. The patient in question was quite unable to obtain any sexual satisfaction or gratification which did not involve his being spanked and humiliated by a woman wearing PVC. In the course of his therapy the genesis of this obsession was traced back to one solitary occasion when as a young child he had been on holiday in London, staying with an unmarried aunt.

For no apparent reason, and for no transgression of which he was aware, she had taken his trousers and underpants off and spanked him on the bare buttocks. He, and no doubt she, had experienced this event sexually. All his subsequent sexual thoughts, feelings, and associations were inextricably bound up in this, as it was, his sexual punishment. In his subsequent sexual development these two powerful themes of sex and punishment became so interlinked they were inseparable. While one may take the view that he is, as a result, a pervert, there can be no doubt that this was a female induced perversion. That is to say that in this case the male's state of perversion was initiated through and responsive toward female sadistic perversion (in this case comparatively mildly expressed). The predilection was acquired.

Moll (1912) observed

> that another factor is in operation here, namely, the fact that the child undergoing punishment is commonly placed across the elder's knees in such a way that pressure upon the child's genital organs is almost unavoidable (Moll, 1912 p320). [49]

In a similar vein, Block comments [50]

> A further attraction is provided by the violent movements and twitchings which affect the parts during chastisement, and which may be regarded as the stimulation of certain movements during coitus.(1938, p329) [51]

Kraft-Ebing in his work Psychopathia Sexualis (Stuttart, 1886) advanced the view that masochism is congenital; that it is a "perversion of uncommonly frequent occurrence" (p 193) and that "the number of masochists is larger than has yet been dreamed".[52] (Admittedly he found this to be the case with male, and female patients - where the sadistic impulse was turned toward the self). Upon considering the evidence presented by Dr Albert (1859) relating to the prevalence of the 'lustful' beating of children on the buttocks, Kraft Ebing commented, "The cases in which lascivious tutors, governesses, etc, cane or spank their pupils without provocation are open to investigation as to the psychological condition of the malfactor".[53]

The fact is however that such maltreatment can give rise to a perverse pleasure, whether this meets a constitutional, or environmentally acquired, sexual impulse.

Freud, in his writings on this theme (which Freud conceded required further development), acknowledged the sadistic disposition of women, and the masochistic inclinations of men.[54]

> It would have been quite impossible to give a clear survey of infantile beating fantasies if I had not limited it, except in one or two connections, to the state of things in females... The little girl beating fantasy passes through three phases, of which the first and third are consciously remembered, the middle one remaining unconscious. The two conscious phases appear to be sadistic, whereas the middle and unconscious one is undoubtedly of a masochistic nature...
>
> For the fact emerges that in their (men's) masochistic fantasies, as well as in the performances they go through for their realisation, they invariably transfer themselves into the part of a woman. that is to say, their masochistic attitude coincides with a feminine one. [55]

Accordingly there would appear to be a complementality of 'perverse disposition' with the forbidden, masculine, sadistic, feminine desire, and the secret feminine, passive, masochistic, masculine wish.

As Freud further observed,

> In her transition to the conscious fantasy (the third phase) which takes the place of the unconscious one, the girl retains the figure of her father, and in that way keeps unchanged the sex of the person beating, so that eventually a man is beating a male child. (That is to say that the male is being beaten, by a female, demonstrably sexually located within the sadistic, masculinity complex).[56]
>
> The boy, on the contrary, changes the figure and sex of the person beating, by putting his mother in the place of his father. but he retains his own figure with the result that the person beating and the person being beaten are of opposite sexes. In the girl what was originally a masochistic (passive) situation is transformed into a sadistic one by means of repression, and its sexual quality is almost effaced. In the case of the boy the situation remains masochistic... She turns herself in fantasy into a man, without herself becoming active in a masculine way, and is no longer anything but a spectator of the event which takes the place of a sexual act. [57]

Evidence for this forbidden, sadistic, masculine impulse in women, generally, and toward children in particular, is highly evident in the accounts of sexually abused men.

Male survivors stories

Richard's story

Given a history of parental marital conflict, Richard was sent to stay with his aunt (aged 28-30).

> ....Things went alright for the first week or so, then she started to smack me for the slightest reason. She always took my trousers or jeans off first, saying she wouldn't waste her energy hitting clothes. Soon after this started, she said I was so naughty, she had to spend most of her day hitting me....she explained that all women have a penis, but that it is only small, if I loved her I would suck it for her. She laid down and made me look at her, with the finger she pointed to her "penis" and gave me instructions how to suck it. She put her hand on top of my head saying she would move it when she wanted me to stop. Of course it never moved, and I knew she pushed me down harder. I felt sure I was going to suffocate and tried to get up. I know now she had an orgasm, but when it happened I thought she'd wee'd in my mouth. That was too much and I threw up all over her thighs. Of course I received a beating, and had to do it again after she had another bath. After this, she would often get me to show her how much I loved her. Sometimes it would be when we were downstairs alone, but most times it would be just before my punishment.[58]

Richard's story clearly demonstrates the inter-relationship between punishment and sexuality, with beating, demonstrated power and domination as integral aspects of the sexual ritual. However a further theme of "public" sexual humiliation also becomes apparent.

> ...One day a friend's daughter stayed with us. She was about a year older than me. While we were upstairs playing, she asked me if I would show her my willy. I am almost certain my aunt was outside the bedroom door, because the instant I took my trousers down, she came in the door with this cane. She made Amanda sit on the bed while I was punished, she told her she would get the same if she ever did anything like that again....[59]
> Sometimes when I told her that I was hard, she would say 'I was being too naughty and to teach me a lesson, I had to go and rape somebody else'. She would then make me go outside. I always sneaked around into the garden shed and sat and cried, terrified of my own erection. I soon found out that masturbating made it go away, on one occasion when she sent me out, she found me in the shed. Without giving me a chance to pull my trousers up, she dragged me up the garden to the house. Her neighbour was in her garden, and she shouted to her, telling her what she had just caught me doing and pointed to my erection. As well as the beating I received, I also had to tell my uncle what I was caught doing. [60]

Tony's story

Tony's story continues the theme of the exercise of feminine sexual power domination and exploitation.

> As near as I can tell, my aunt started to molest me about the age of three. At about that time, I had to sleep with her since we did not have enough beds. The abuse continued until the age of about six and a half, when my mother found out and stopped it, as well as making different sleeping arrangements for me. I was molested virtually every night during that time. She made me perform oral sex on her, held me on top of her and caused my small penis to penetrate her as much as it could. She taught me how to hump. During the day since we had only one bathroom and she was in charge of me, she would go into the bathroom with me most of the time. She would sit on the toilet and open her legs to allow me to urinate into the toilet between them. When I finished, she would rub my penis in her vagina and attempt to get it erect....[61]

Supporting the central premise of this paper Tony goes on to comment,

> I guess I will be in therapy for the rest of my life. I know the experts say that female sexual abuse is rare. Don't believe it - there are many out there like me who were abused and who are now causing more abuse. In the support group I attend, 75% of the molesters have been abused by women and some have been abused by men and women.[62]

Alan's story

As a child during the war, Alan had been evacuated and was sent to live with an aunt (Amy) who would have been aged "around 30".

> Amy's daughter was a year older than myself. Amy was in the habit of spanking her daughter over her knee and shortly after I was moved there she started spanking me. Once when over her knee she put her hand on my penis and said 'It's getting hard, come and look at this'. My aunt Maggie came in and they rubbed my penis until it was sore. I certainly don't remember having an erection. One day I was spanked in front of the American (Amy's boyfriend). I cannot remember what for and he suggested to the women that I be made to wear Amy's daughter's knickers as part of the punishment. I was ten years old. From then until I was thirteen I was constantly 'abused' by the two women, usually with the man present and watching. I kissed and licked their nipples and vagina, they stroked my penis. I was always spanked, probably every day...
> Amy's daughter was also spanked every day, but was not present while the women touched me. Once when caught listening at the door, she was whipped with a cane and tied to the toilet. Both of us were spanked in front of visitors, who sometimes joined in. One of them was a fiancee of my uncle who was visiting. She became my aunt. She was extremely

religious. She invited me for 'tea' at her own house, and while I was there she spanked me for herself, nude. Afterwards she gave me a bath. [63]

In *Philip's story* a clear linkage is made between childhood sexual abuse and psychological and emotional disturbance.

> I came back home to my mother when I was about four years old, having been evacuated to my Grandmother's because of the war. My mother used to trap me in the bedroom and get me to do things to her. When I was fourteen my mother used to come into my bed in the early hours of the morning, arouse me sexually, and sexual intercourse would take place.... I know a lot of damage was done by the emotional abuse, that really screwed me up. [64]

Henry's story (Written with Henry as the third person subject, indicating the writer's need to distance himself from the realities of his own abuse - understandably)

> Someone reports two women and a child in bed - the male child giving the faint touch of masculinity the women wanted, but without the full aura of horror that an adult male aroused in the women's minds....as the third country Christmas approached, the child was playing by a dangerous window in Iris' bedroom and she beat him so hard his thigh was smashed... Iris' son was raped by other adults connected with his school but, although she could see his injuries, she refused to protect him by transferring him to a different school. Her son learned that mothers were not safe - they not only abused, but also colluded with others who abused. He was isolated and vulnerable. [65]

Peter's story (of his mother). This involved sexual domination to the point were Peter was denied control over his own body.

> If I protested about sleeping with her, she humiliated me verbally...
> Gradually the message became clear. I was to kiss and hug her the way she liked or I would be punished yet again. When I slept with her, I would curl up, put my hands between my thighs and try to protect myself, both from the cold and from her. She would bring her right arm over my body and remove my hands, touching me on the thighs. She never allowed me to control my own body and I found it profoundly disturbing... During my childhood mother also found reasons to stuff medicine up my bottom and abused me in other ways. There were erotic consequences to many of her actions and to the physical punishments she meted out. [66]

Peter's story

> Day by day, Mum pinched, punched or pushed a finger hard up my arse, she ripped the life out of me. [67]

72

Paul's story exemplifies significantly the impact of both physical punishment and psychological abuse, which can be equally, if not more, damaging.

> She genitally interfered with me and tried to make me meet her overwhelming need for attention and love.... I think I became her substitute penis... She tried to suffocate me, used to beat me in frustrated rage at her life and she used to tie me up... Control and dominance of me was very important to her and resistance was met with violence from beatings with canes to harsh verbal stabs.[68]

These accounts of maternal and female abuse crucially contradict the conventional wisdom regarding the nature of possible "masculine", sadistic, feminine sexuality. Dominated as it is by the medical profession and psychiatrists in particular, the sexual reality of femininity is proscribed from understanding, or perhaps more accurately from conscious possibility.

Storr comments,

> In clinical practice, at any rate, it is not uncommon to find intensely masochistic women who desire to be subjugated, beaten, and ill treated before they become erotically aroused: but it is rare to find women who actually want to beat or ill treat men in order to obtain erotic satisfaction.[69]

Clearly where the experienced sadistic impulse is denied expression or discharge, it may undergo psychical transformation, being turned or redirected toward the self in masochistic form, however it disguises the essentially sadistic impulse. Storr's analysis apparently failed to comprehend that accounts of masochism from his female patients were descriptions of a defensive psychical postures: they represent the mechanism employed to disguise and defend against the experienced forbidden, masculine, sadistic impulse, by introjecting it as an acceptable, feminine, passive (masochistic) drive.

What was taking place between Storr and these female patients was extraordinarily complex, involving societal and gender imperatives, individual personal socialisation, and a psychical exchange involving transference and counter-transference. All of these factors contributed in an essential misunderstanding by both therapist and patient as to the real nature of the problem, which, clearly, is central to its resolution.

These were not so much accounts of treatment, but descriptions of a process of the mutual reaffirmation of gender stereotype, which if anything only served to amplify, or to assist and collude in the disguise of the crucial problem.

The success of females in disguising the real nature of their forbidden (masculine, sadistic) sexual impulse, is delightfully exemplified by Gibson, in his comments relating to the "sadistic female".

"We may agree, I believe that the whole thing is a male fantasy".[70]

Precisely who is living in a "fantasy" is a point of contention, which is centrally questioned by this and other contemporary papers.

Notes

1   See Mason, op. cit.
2   See Kaplan, op. cit. Chapter 12, *The Child as Salvation,* p. 408-452.
3   Based on the scenario as outlined by Freud, New Introductory Lectures, op cit. p. 87.
4   Kaplan, op. cit, pp. 199/200.
5   Kraft-Ebing, op. cit, provides an interesting case study exemplifying this phenomenon, Case 84, p. 224.
6   Jung, C. G. (1971) *The Collected Works*, Ed Read, Fordan and Adier, Vol Vl Psychological Types, Routledge Kegan and Paul, London, plo (11).
7   Jung, C. G. (1972) *Four Archetypes*, Routledge, Kegan and Paul, London, pp. 16/17.
8   Kaplan, L. J. op. cit. p. 454.
9   Barty, K. op. cit. p. 189.
10   Freud, S. *An Infantile Neurosis and Other Works*, Ed. Strachey, J. et al, Hogart Press, London, p. 129-132.
11   See Douglas, J. D. et al, (1980) *Introduction to the Sociologies of Everyday Life*, Allyn and Bacon Inc, Boston, p. 155-181 (Toward a Complex Universe: Existential Sociology).
12   Sartre, J. P. (1962) *Existential Psychoanalysis* S H Regency, Chicago.
13   Edwards, D. G. (1982) *Existential Psychotherapy*, The Process of Caring, Gardner Press, NewYork.
14   Yalom, I. D. (1982) *Existential Psychotherapy*, Basic Books, New York.
15   Freud, S. *New Introductory Lectures*, op. cit. p. 74.
16   Kaplan, L. J. op. cit. p. 456.
17   Kaplan, L. K. op. cit. p. 401.
18   Friday, N. op. cit. p. 43.
19   Friday, N. op. cit. p. 94.
20   Friday, N. op. cit. p. 56.
21   Friday, N. op. cit. p.56.
22   Friday, N. op. cit. p. 56.
23   Elliot, M. (1993) Ed. Female Sexual Abuse of Children, The Ultimate Taboo, Longman, Essex, p. 23.
24   Ibid, p. 8.
25   Ibid, Sgroi and Sargent, p. 19.
26   Ibid, Hunter, pp. 45/47.
27   Ibid, Eleanor's story, pp. 128/129.
28   Ibid, Lynne's story, pp. 130/137.
29   Ibid, Lynne's story, p. 131.
30   Ibid, Lynne's story, p. 132.
31   Ibid, Karen's story, pp. 145/146
32   Ibid, Karen's story, p. 145.

33	Ibid, Karen's story, p. 145.
34	Ibid, Karen's story, p, 146.
35	Ibid, Gillian's story, pp. 147/148.
36	Ibid, p. 147.
37	Ibid, p. 147.
38	Ibid, p. 147.
39	Ibid, p. 147.
40	Ibid, Rachael's story, pp. 148/157.
41	Ibid, p. 155 .
42	Ibid, Sarah's story, pp. 161/165.
43	Ibid, p. 162.
44	Faller, K. op. cit. pp. 263-272.
45	Quintano, I. M. (1992) Case profiles of early childhood abuse *Treating Abuse Today* 2, 11-13, p. 13.
46	Morris, D. (1967) *The Naked Ape*, Corgi Books, p. 147.
47	Freud, S. Vol XVII, op. cit. p. 198.
48	Rousseau, J. J. (1954) *Confessions*, Penguin Books, London, p. 26.
49	Moll, A. (1912) The Sexual Life of the Child, translated by Dr M E Paul, Berlin.
50	Bloch, I. (1938) Sexual Life in England Past and Present, London.
51	Kraft-Ebing, R. (1886) *Psychopathis Sexualis* Stuttgart.
52	Ibid.
53	Ibid.
54	Freud, S. Vol XVII, op. cit. p. 198/199.
55	Ibid.
56	Ibid.
57	Kaplan, L. op. cit.
58	Elliot, M. op. cit. Richard's story.
59	Ibid.
60	Ibid.
61	Ibid, Tony's story.
62	Ibid.
63	Ibid, Alan's story.
64	Ibid, Philip's story.
65	Ibid, Henry's story.
66	Ibid, Peter's story.
67	Ibid.
68	Ibid, Paul's story.
69	Storr, A. (1989) *Freud* Oxford University Press, Oxford.
70	Ibid.

8 The mask slips. Female child sexual abuse

One of the most revolutionary exposés of child sex abuse and the sexual abuse of children by females centred upon the McMartin Pre-school facility, Manhattan Beach, California.[1] This was a prestigious middle class facility with ostensibly ordinary respectable teachers and ancillary staff.[2] The fact that it was the scene of ritual sexual abuse for hundreds of three, four and five year old children shocked America.[3] US authorities saw the number of child sexual abuse cases in day care settings rise from 7,000 in 1975 to 120,000 ten years later.[4]

This led to a two year nationwide investigation of sexual abuse in day care, which graphically demonstrated the reality of child sexual abuse by females.[5] Something which had perhaps previously been regarded, in the public mind at least, as the sole preserve of "male perverts".

It is implicitly contended in this paper that the uncovery of the extent of female sexual abuse in day care will be a prelude to similar findings in family contexts.

With regard to multiple perpetrators involving "pornography, ritualistic practice, extended and bizarre abuse" over protracted periods of time, and children suffering "the most serious and lasting damage".[6] "Three quarters involved both male and female perpetrators, 17% just females and only 9% males. In the 74% of these cases victims included both boys and girls." During the study it had been assumed that males had been the initiators who encouraged the participation of females. However further investigation led to the conclusion that females "played active if not initiatory roles". [7] Significantly for this paper in relation to multiple perpetrators, it was noted that the "mother son abuser combination was particularly common".[8]

Contrary to previous research findings which implicate men much more than women in child sexual abuse, as reviewed by Finkelhor and Russell 1984,[9] Finkelhor's (1988) findings of sexual abuse in day care noted a higher incidence of female involvement. [10]

Finkelhor reported that in 270 cases, there were 147 female perpetrators. Of some 293 boys sexually abused, 59% were abused by at least one woman. Of the 471 girls sexually abused 50% were abused by women.[11]

Disconcertingly it was also reported that the female abusers were "more respectable" than their male counterparts, and were more likely to hold a high school Diploma or Degree.[12]

Interestingly for this research "women were significantly more likely to abuse younger children, a tendency which has also been reported by Faller (1987)".[13] Finkelhor also reached the conclusion that "female perpetrators" were significantly more likely than men to have forced children to sexually abuse others, and to have participated in ritualistic mass abuse".[14]

Finkelhor's perhaps unique contribution to the literature and research on this subject goes some way to vindicate the view that women (in common with men) may regard young children as sexually attractive and desirable, and given the opportunity this may find expression in sexual contact, abuse and worse as documented.[15]

Mathews made a similar contribution to the literature on female sexual offenders when he commented in relation to Canada (based upon his assumption that some 10% of sex abusers are female).

...if one in seven Canadian men and one in four women were sexually abused as a child, as a study has indicated, that works out to about five million people. Ten percent of that figure would mean 500,000 Canadians have been abused by girls of women; one per cent would mean about 50,000. I don't know about you, but that doesn't seem like a minor number... (The Globe and Mail, 30 October 1991).

Finkelhor and Russell (1984) arrived at the conclusion, based upon their research, that females were the perpetrators in fourteen per cent of the cases against boys, and in six per cent of the cases against girl victims of child sexual abuse.

The National Incidence (1981) Study reported that 13% of female sexual abuse victims and twenty-four per cent of male sexual abuse victims stated that they had been abused by a female. (However, methodological deficiencies were identified in this data).

These findings also support the Freudian thesis that all individuals are potentially attracted to children, and that it is social conditioning, internalised societal norms, and social proscription which frustrate the sexual enactment of primal desires in this regard [16] (which in turn creates ego, super-ego conflict). Given the universal nature of the human experience, variations in the normality or exceptionality of female/child sexual abuse may be centrally influenced by a given culture's willingness to accept that
(1)   this form of abuse does take place, and that
(2)   this form of abuse is a relatively common phenomenon.

In Japan, for example, it has been suggested that mother/son incest is the predominant form of child sexual abuse.[17]

La Fontaine reports one hospital case where a mother from another country and culture would kiss her young boys' genitals. She viewed this as expressing affection. The hospital staff took the view that this practice should stop with the elder boy at least as it could lead to abuse.[18] (The response to a male parent similarly involved with his daughter, may be inferred).

Olson reports the cultural normality of Turkish women who admire and touch the genitals of young children without inhibition.[19]

In his Northern Ireland research involving sexually abusing mothers, Reid provides the following two accounts.[20]

> I'm coming to the abuse or what I thought was abuse that I caused in my child's life. I saw him doing something that I felt he could not know about unless someone was doing it to him. He was pulling at himself in the bath. What happened was that he was being abused by someone, I thought I had abused him and I was trying to find out, I drifted back to my own abuse. When it happened I spent four or five days to get settled, if I have abused him what will I do. He was playing with himself and he had never done this before, this time he was doing something he should not have been doing. He was trying to touch me down there, how could he know and I thought what if he touched me down there what does that do for a person for a child to touch someone that way, why does anyone do it, are they getting something in the course of thinking this, the child touched me down there and I was sure I had abused him. When it came to mind I nearly went mad. I rang rape crisis and asked what they thought. Then I thought back to how I used to rub his private parts in an affectionate way. All the women in our family did this, my granny, my mum, my sister. Then I thought this gives someone the opening to abuse. I tried to hide my sexual feelings so no one would be at risk. I'm frightened to touch my children. I could not cope with the thought that I was sexually attracted to children.[21]

A second abusing mother reported,

> You know I think I loved the children because I could abuse them. I'm holding back here, but I'll try. I abused Julie since she was 2 months old, I loved it. The more I abused her the more I needed to abuse. I knew she could tell no one, I could do whatever I liked and I did. I did the same when the boys came along. I had sex with the boys and Julie and eventually I'd make the boys abuse Julie. They didn't want to but I'd punish them until they did.[22]

The child protection agency, Kidscape, report more than one hundred victims of sexual abuse on their files.[23] Michael Elliot observed that while official estimates of female sexual abuse account for 5% of all sexual abuse, a truer figure may be 20%.[24] Cianne Longdon, a psychotherapist specialising in child sexual abuse reports that half her private patients during the past five years, and half of those she has seen at a local centre have been abused by women.[25] Kidscape characterise their experience of child sexual abuse by females as follows.

> Girls may have objects inserted into their vaginas, whereas little boys may be taken to the parental bed where fondling and oral sex can take place. One patient reported objects as diverse as rose stems and bottles being inserted. "Judith" was sexually abused from infancy, forced to perform

oral sex and was violently penetrated with objects. "Tony" was sexually molested by an aunt from the age of three and was encouraged to perform sexual intercourse by the age of six and a half. [26]

In her classic work Weldon [27] cites a particularly bizarre case involving a young boy placed in the care of an aunt, who not only made him wear girls clothing, but insisted that he behave like a girl. He was treated in this fashion from three years of age and was subsequently sent to a girls school. At the age of twelve his mother realised what was happening, took him away from the aunt, severely punished him and sent him to an all boys school. This was doomed not to work and eventually he was returned to his aunt at whose hands he suffered "denigration for his maleness". [28]

In Britain Childline was established as a charity in 1986. It invited children who were subject to abuse to make contact offering a confidential "helpline". During their first year of operation (during a three month period in 1987) "nearly 2/5 of boys reporting sexual abuse accused women, nearly half accused their own mothers and a small proportion other female relatives". [29]

Research undertaken in Northern Ireland (RVH, QUB) Child Sexual Abuse in Northern Ireland [30], established that "some 298 (90.3%) of girls were abused by a male while 4 (1.2%) were abused by a female" [31]. They too however encountered the phenomenon of co-abuse which they found "disturbing". "The 37 (9.1%) children who were subjected to this type of abuse also experienced some of the more penetrative types of sexual abuse. Six children were abused by both parents and in another six the mothers were the co-abusers". They conclude, "although in the study the vast majority of children were abused by males, more attention needs to be directed toward the problem of female abusers". [32]

Female/child sexual perversion

Limitations to disclosure, uncovery and resolution

Gender typing and stereotyping goes beyond how we treat and describe people, to become powerful forces of human designation and regulation, which become internalised, ultimately impinging upon, or even determining, i.e. psyche of the individual. Demands for conformity become so powerful that departures from convention are not anticipated. While we are beginning to acquire data which more accurately measures the extent and nature of female sexual abuse with children, this aspect of female sexuality still remains virtually a closed book.

Not that this is the fault of women, the blame being located within a universal gender conspiracy with an imperative of idealising women, which they (women) internalise and feel compelled to act out, leaving a psychically dangerous fault line between this virtual (socially ascribed) and actual (internally determined) identity.

This combination of sociological and psychological circumstance has resulted in failure, our failure to fully understand women and women's failure to understand themselves, such is the inherent contradiction of the position in which we (society) have placed them.

As Weldon comments, "we have all become silent conspirators in a system in which change could not be envisaged since no one would acknowledge that such behaviour existed".[33] This is reminiscent of Kincaid's observation "not six people now alive will openly admit to being sexually aroused to spanking children, among the several billion who are".[34] This quotation does actually make a serious point in relation to social taboo, and resistance toward uncovery. Female/child sexual abuse is unthinkable precisely because, under the social construction of reality thesis we choose to conceptualise of "the problem" as unthinkable, preferring to employ the mechanism of denial. However the real failure lies in our apparent studied inability to observe, listen and learn, nonjudgementally and empathetically to what some women want and need to tell us, if only we give them permission. This involves the realisation that their disclosure places us in a very privileged position and should be responded to with compassion and humility. As Weldon observes, "This failure (to recognise the 'problem') has deprived some women of a better understanding of their difficulties".[35]

In Western society it would appear that we have virtually sanitised extreme female sexuality and perversion, or assigned it to the brothel and to pornography. It is as if perversion, for so long acknowledged as a masculine phenomenon, has been disallowed women. As Weldon protests, "there is still no acknowledgement of female perversion"[36]...."Two decades on we are similarly failing to admit the possibility of maternal incest".[37]

Women find it very difficult to talk about their own sexuality, and sexual needs, not to mention their own "perversions", drives and impulses. I recall one patient saying, "I'm sorry for you men. We (women) keep on giving you such contradictory messages. It's because we don't know what we want ourselves. We suffer from sexual identity conflicts".

Women are instinctually driven by very powerful primitive sexual impulses, which are arguably more encompassing and poignant than those experienced by men. However, as a result of socialisation, conditioning, gender typing and "ascribed virtuously", they become impailed in both conflict and entrapment.

For a mother to admit to having sexual feelings for her child, is to risk being labelled and stigmatised as a pervert.[38]

It is all too obvious that women experiencing such feelings and emotions fear being misunderstood most of all.

As Weldon comments upon the basis of her professional experience,

The more I have listened to women, fumbling, usually in the dark, with their special problem, the more convinced I have become that as a caring society we need to bridge the large gap which exists between what we already know of female sexuality and the full truth about women and the vicissitudes of their sexual experience.[39]

Notes

1   Finkelhor, D., Williams, L., Burns, N., (1988) *Nursery Crimes. Sexual Abuse in Day Care,* Sage, California, p. 1.
2   Ibid, p. 41.
3   Ibid, p. 8.
4   Ibid, p. 10.
5   Ibid, p. 41.
6   Ibid, p. 45.
7   Ibid, p. 39.
8   Ibid, p. 39.
9   Finkelhor, D. and Russell, D.(1984) *Women as Perpetrators:* Review of the evidence In D Finkelhor (ed), *Child Sexual Abuse.* New theory and research (p. 171-187), Beverly Hills, California, Sage.
10   Finkelhor, D. et al, op. cit. p. 40.
11   Ibid, p. 40.
12   Ibid, p. 41.
13   Faller, K. (1987)*Women Who Sexually Abuse Children.* Violence and Victims, 2:4, 263-276.
14   Finkelhor, D. et al, op. cit. p. 435.
15   Finkelhor, D. et al, op. cit.
16   Freud, S. (1975) *Totem and Taboo and Other Works* - Totem and Taboo, The Horror of Incest. Ed. J Strachey et al, Vol. XIII 1913-14, Hogarth Press, London, p. 1-7.
17   Personal communication from M Lock, an anthropologist working in Japan, recorded by Jean La Fontaine, in *Child Sexual Abuse* (below), p. 106.
18   La Fontaine, J. (1990) *Child Sexual Abuse*, Basil Blackwell Inc., Oxford, p. 106.
19   Olson, E. A. (1981) Socio exonomic and psycho-cultural context of child abuse in Turkey, in J E Corbin (Ed), *Child Abuse and Neglect: Cross Cultural Perspectives,* University of California Press, Berkeley, p. 108.
20   Reid, M. (1992) *Female Sexual Abuse,* Unpublished dissertation, Faculty of Social and Health Sciences, University of Ulster.
21   Ibid, p. 55.
22   Ibid, p. 61.
23   *Observer, News Section,* (1.3.92) "Child Sexual Abuse by Females Alarms Welfare Agencies."
24   Ibid.
25   Ibid.
26   Ibid.
27   Weldon, op. cit. p. 77.
28   Weldon, op. cit. p. 77.
29   La Fontaine, J. (1990) *Child Sexual Abuse,* Polity Press, Cambridge, p. 107-108.
30   The Research Team, QUB/RVH, (1990) Child Sexual Abuse in Northern Ireland. *A Research Study of Incidence.* Greystone Book, Antrim.

31 Ibid, p. 63.
32 Ibid, p. 89.
33 Weldon, op. cit. p. 16.
34 Kincaid, J. (1993) *Child Loving.* The Erotic Child and Victorian Cultures. Routledge, London, p. 426.
35 Weldon, op. cit. p. 16.
36 Weldon, op. cit. p. 5.
37 Weldon, op. cit. p. 10.
38 See Lees, S. (1993) *Sugar and Spice, Sexuality and Adsolescent Girls.* Penguin, London, p. 227-260.
    Weldon, op. cit. p. 10.
39 Weldon, op. cit.

9 Dimensions of maternal sexuality

Freud has suggested that our evolution from primal man, to "civilized" man is a transition which has taken place in a relatively short space of time, and that the demands of civilization on our essentially primal psyche comes at a great psychical cost; repression and its associated symptoms.[1]

Freud has also taught us that the psychical or psychological development of women is both more complex and traumatic for them, than for men.[2] The following visual formulation will suggest that for some women a further psychical (internal) vs socially proscribed (external) paradox is to be encountered. This involves those women who find themselves attracted to, and desirous of sexual contact with, their own infants, in which the only outcome would appear to be conflict. This is potentially a sensitive and difficult aspect of what is, for some mothers, the reality of the maternal experience. The following material carries implications for a greater awareness of this phenomenon in professional practice, and toward the need for increased social and professional understanding.

Maternal management of infantile sexuality psychical consequences for the mother

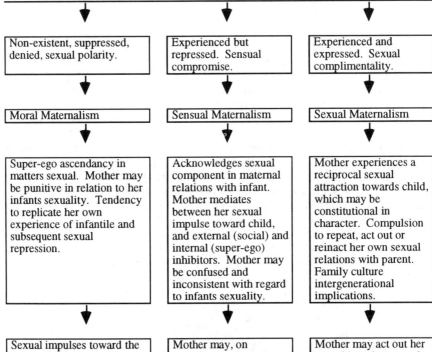

Infant develops intensive sexual interest in mother (constitutionally determined) of pathological proportions [3]

Maternal sexual orientation toward child

Non-existent, suppressed, denied, sexual polarity.	Experienced but repressed. Sensual compromise.	Experienced and expressed. Sexual complimentality.
Moral Maternalism	Sensual Maternalism	Sexual Maternalism
Super-ego ascendancy in matters sexual. Mother may be punitive in relation to her infants sexuality. Tendency to replicate her own experience of infantile and subsequent sexual repression.	Acknowledges sexual component in maternal relations with infant. Mother mediates between her sexual impulse toward child, and external (social) and internal (super-ego) inhibitors. Mother may be confused and inconsistent with regard to infants sexuality.	Mother experiences a reciprocal sexual attraction towards child, which may be constitutional in character. Compulsion to repeat, act out or reinact her own sexual relations with parent. Family culture intergenerational implications.
Sexual impulses toward the child undergo repression, and fail to find expression, creating psychical conflict. The mother child relationship may be characterised by a coldness or correctness	Mother may, on occasion, act upon her sexual impulse toward child, which may create quilt and confusion. Struggles valiantly with drives and proscriptions - and with what is, and what is not, appropriate touch, with a consequence of guilt.	Mother may act out her sexual impulse toward child. This may be seen as natural, within cultural norms of family, or may give rise to enormous guilt, conflict and distress.

Maternal management of infantile sexuality:

A typology of responses and the inferred psychical consequences for the child

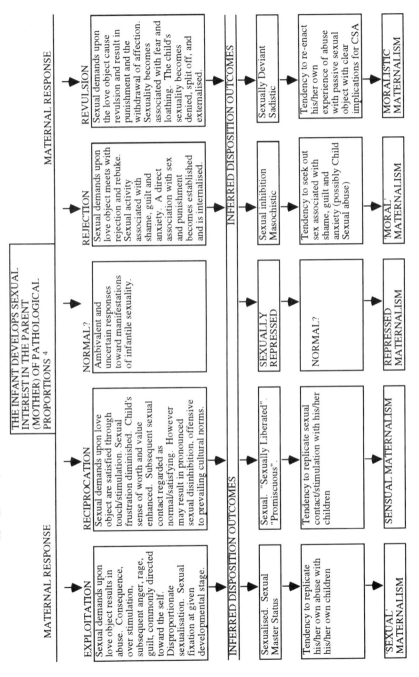

	THE INFANT DEVELOPS SEXUAL INTEREST IN THE PARENT (MOTHER) OF PATHOLOGICAL PROPORTIONS [4]			
MATERNAL RESPONSE				**MATERNAL RESPONSE**
EXPLOITATION Sexual demands upon love object results in abuse. Consequence, over stimulation, subsequent anger, rage, guilt, commonly directed toward the self. Disproportionate sexualisation. Sexual fixation at given developmental stage.	**RECIPROCATION** Sexual demands upon love object are satisfied through touch/stimulation. Sexual frustration diminished. Child's sense of worth and value enhanced. Subsequent sexual contact regarded as normal/satisfying. However may result in pronounced sexual disinhibition, offensive to prevailing cultural norms.	**NORMAL?** Ambivalent and uncertain responses toward manifestations of infantile sexuality.	**REJECTION** Sexual demands upon love object meets with rejection and rebuke. Sexual activity associated with shame, guilt and anxiety. A direct association with sex and punishment becomes established and is internalised.	**REVULSION** Sexual demands upon the love object cause revulsion and result in punishment and the withdrawal of affection. Sexuality becomes associated with fear and loathing. The child's sexuality becomes denied, split off, and externalised.
INFERRED DISPOSITION OUTCOMES	**INFERRED DISPOSITION OUTCOMES**		**INFERRED DISPOSITION OUTCOMES**	
Sexualised. Sexual Master Status	Sexual. "Sexually Liberated". "Promiscuous".	**SEXUALLY REPRESSED**	Sexual inhibition Masochistic	Sexually Deviant Sadistic
Tendency to replicate his/her own abuse with his/her own children	Tendency to replicate sexual contact/stimulation with his/her children	**NORMAL?**	Tendency to seek out sex associated with shame, guilt and anxiety (possibly Child Sexual abuse)	Tendency to re-enact his/her own experience of abuse with passive sexual object with clear implications for CSA
'SEXUAL' MATERNALISM	**SENSUAL MATERNALISM**	**REPRESSED MATERNALISM**	**'MORAL' MATERNALISM**	**MORALISTIC MATERNALISM**

(Accordingly the theme of relative neuroticism, as documented by Freud in his femininity lecture, may be further psychically complicated for women, as mothers, impaled upon the above meta-psychological paradox.[5]) The material presented thus far in this chapter is clearly controversial and debatable, however it does go some way in pointing out the variability, and significantly the inferred consequences of the early maternal relationship. An important theme which emerged in thinking through maternal responses and their developmental consequences was that the "socially correct" and "moral" responses to child sexuality are potentially psychologically devastating for the individuals concerned. And yet we know that such approaches to child management are not uncommon, or rather that they are normal. Psychiatrists, psychotherapists and social workers work with the legacy of such "moral maternalism" on a daily basis. Similarly the exploitation of children, with the associated consequence of the sexualised child carries, a potential for the destruction, even self mutilation and self destruction, of the individual.

Within the presented continuum this leaves us with a further two maternal response categories. Normal, a generalisation, which almost defies quantification, and which may involve elements of maternal response across the presented spectrum.

Finally we have the reciprocal model of response which accepts that, the child is sexually demanding, and has sexual needs; and that the mother is not a clinical, but human and sexual being who may instinctively (driven by primal sexual forces) (1) recognise her child's sexuality and (2) respond to her child's sexual demands sensitivity and lovingly. Clearly this may involve what may be characterised as sexual contact or sexual abuse. This can involve a massive conflict in many mothers torn by the experienced sexual impulse towards their child, and internalised super-ego, and social proscription.

Many theorists have alluded to a sensual dimension in the early maternal environment. Winnicott's "primary maternal preoccupation", and the "intensely private incommunicado between mother and child"[6] and Sullivan wrote of mother/child "empathy", and "emotional communion".[7] Suttie viewed the quality of this primary relationship as being so important he wrote of the taboo on tenderness endemic in our culture.[8] (In terms of this paper 'moral maternalism') Brown has written of "the mutually caressing relationship of child and mother".[9]

It is being contended here that early mother child sensual and even "sexual" contact and or stimulation in an emotionally secure and loving context is psychically and developmentally preferable to the "moral maternalism" which is presented as normal by the state and its institutions, particularly social work departments. However this paper would not go so far as to agree with Shengold, when in the light of the above he was driven to question "is the sexualisation of the craving for human contact that can lead to incest and perversion a healthier turn (for the child) than the arrest of emotional and sexual development".[10] However the "soul murder" which he cites can be related to the "moral maternalism" referred to in this paper, involving the rejection of, and responses of revulsion toward, infantile sexuality with all its consequences.

As noted previously we have very little collective knowledge about the reality of female sexuality.[11] Evidence has been provided in previous chapters to assert the fact that some women are sexually attracted to small children, and that in certain contexts, are more likely than men to sexually co-abuse them, and to sadistically, and ritually sexually abuse them (which in the typology advanced in this paper may be linked to their maternal childhood experience of sexual exploitation).

Previous chapters also documented evidence to attest to the fact that some women are sexually attracted to their own children. Weldon has referred to this as "perverse motherhood" but in so doing she falls into the sociological dilemma she criticises so effectively, which centres upon the stereotyping and labelling of women.[12]

Rather we should take the view as advocated by Freud, that all adults are sexually attracted to children, and that we are inhibited only by internalised social proscription. Social proscription is there, obviously for very valid reasons, and must be maintained. However it is being advocated here that a much greater liberalism must be shown toward women who experience a sexual attraction toward their young children in the early years of life.

If the feminine sexual impulse toward children is perceived of as perverse and unnatural, it will tend to be both concealed, and enacted, perversely. When the line of perversion is crossed, and the taboo rendered neutral in its effect, gratificational exploitation, as documented, is likely to become both sadistic and extreme, and may not even take account of age. As Weldon states "My clinical observations show that mothers who display perverse tendencies toward their off-spring do so within the first two years of a child's life".[13]

Freud has demonstrated that this tendency is natural and instinctively driven, and the opening flow chart in this chapter suggests that its expression, or its repression, leads to psychical conflict. This places women who experience a sexual attraction toward their infants (responsively or otherwise) in the most difficult situation, which is likely to be grossly misunderstood even by professionals, or perhaps most of all by professionals.

Society cannot go on imposing expectations of women and mothers as "virtuous madonnas". Women and mothers must be given the permission to (1) recognise their true sexuality and not that version of sexuality which is ascribed to them, (2) discuss their sexuality and sexual drives with informed professionals who will understand, and not label and discount them, and (3) to bring the realities of the parameters of female sexuality, into the public arena. As Weldon observes, "We help neither her or her children, nor society in general, if we glorify motherhood so blindly as to exclude the fact that some mothers can act perversely".[14] Incredibly this involves the recognition of a reality which even highly trained professionals choose to deny, or not accept, often for highly complex reasons.[15]

Reid's Northern Ireland study gives an account of one abusing mother who had sought professional help.[16] She was "keen that her story should be used to improve social work and medical intervention in this area, as she had suffered a life time of despair and tragedy because of ill informed and misguided interventions from both professions"[17] (i.e. medical and social work).

Another of Reid's respondents who felt at risk of sexually abusing her child reported her experience of seeking professional help.

She recalls vividly trying to get help shortly after meeting her future husband at 17. (She already had one child, Julie, at that time). On disclosing her story to her GP she was given some pills and told to forget it. At 23 she told another GP and was told that it was no big deal and that quite a bit of it was in her imagination. At 27 she confided in a hospital doctor in a plea for help to be told that she must have got something out of it. She was so devastated to be told this that she felt that she must be to blame for it all and she attempted suicide before again being admitted to a psychiatric hospital. [18]

Presumably if professional staff, both social work and medical, were more inclined to regard this as a natural, human, and not uncommon phenomenon, the entire ethos of treatment, and outcome would have been different.

Fay Weldon comments, "Everyone is ready to recognise paternal incest, which as far as we know is much more common, but not what mothers do. Nobody believes it is happening - sometimes even to the mother's chagrin".[19]

The disturbing fact is that even mother-son incest can be taking place in cases actively being worked on by professionals however "it is interesting how often maternal incest comes to light only when the children begin to show open violence".[20]

In accounting for the differential uncovery of father/daughter incest, relative to mother/son incest Shengold questioned, "It is because most psychiatrists are male and have a deep resistance to the uncovering or the publication of the fulfilment of the male's characteristic forbidden oedipal wish".[21]

Another explanation could lie in the fact that many professionals believe that intervention is dysfunctional for the family involved and particularly for the victim. This may have been consolidated through recent accounts of children being abused by staff in children's homes, by media and other accounts of children abusing other children while in care.

A further explanation impinging upon professionals of both sexes is the residue of unresolved feelings about sexuality within their own childhood experience.

Many professionals harbour inhibitions privately when faced with intimate, often disturbing or unpalatable sexual details, especially involving young children. These inhibitions may arise from unresolved feelings about our own sexuality or sexual relationships or may reawaken memories of personally experienced abuse. [22]

As professionals we need to be much more open to female sexuality generally and maternal sexuality in particular and resist the temptation to take seriously only that material which conforms to our stereotypes of, the feminine, and the maternal.

As Freud wrote in 1898

But an important consideration comes into play here - namely that a Doctor who is experienced in these things (concealed sexual life) does not meet his patients unprepared and as a rule does not have to ask them for information but only for a confirmation of his surmises ...

It would undoubtedly spur such people on to abandon their secretiveness from the moment they have made up their minds to seek help for their sufferings. Moreover, it is in the interests of all of us that a higher degree of honesty about sexual things should become a duty among men and women than has hitherto been expected of them. This cannot be anything but a gain for sexual morality. In matters of sexuality we are at present, every one of us, ill or well, nothing but hypocrites. It will be to all our good if, as a result of such general honesty, a certain amount of toleration in sexual concerns should be attained. [23]

While Freud asserted (initially) the fact of father daughter incest, and suffered accordingly, the taboo which surrounds maternal sexual abuse, contemporaneously, is arguably even stronger. As Lawson (1993) observes,

Clinicians and researchers are not immune toward the abhorrent emotional reactions toward violation of the incest taboo. Banning (1989)[24] suggests that the current cultural bias against recognising mother-son sexual abuse is reminiscent of Freud's struggle to convince a disbelieving audience in 1896 of the possibility of father-daughter incest among his female patients. [25]

The forces of resistance toward uncovery or exposure are pervasive and formidable. As Bass (1991) comments "many young men would rather face execution that admit that they were sexually abused". [26] Lewis, Malloug and Webb (1989) provide us with a literal example of this. [27]

This resistance to disclose the reality of maternal and female sexual abuse, is perhaps understandable, given the current state of ignorance, which can inform responses to children so abused.

Tony, a male child upon reporting his sexual abuse by an aunt to his mother.

She questioned me and beat the hell out of me when I told her what had gone on, although I never really told her just what had happened or how extensive the abuse had been. [28]

Lynne, when telling her teachers,

I was threatened not to tell anything that went on in our house; but age ten, I attempted to tell the nun who was my catechism teacher. She slapped me across the face telling me never to lie, and to honour my parents. [29]

Jane, who was subjected to perverse mothering, comments,

The psychiatrist who saw me could find no signs of mental illness, apart from the fact that I was 'a bit neurotic', he said. He exclaimed I was a creative genius (whatever that means) but how could I create anything if I could express my feelings. A social worker told me I was a delinquent and a nuisance to my nice parents, who had been interviewed by the psychiatrist. No professional diagnosed abuse in childhood, let alone sexual abuse from a woman.[30]

While we are obviously lacking in a sexual and social knowledge of female sexuality, our deficiency is perhaps most pronounced in not having a theoretical or conceptual framework which makes particular female sexual behaviours, comprehensible.

The accounts of maternal and female sexual abuse, presented in this text may be viewed as random phenomena, or as having a locatedness in the meta-psychopathological development of women. This latter approach is advanced in the following chapter.

Notes

1   Freud, S. (1975) *Anxiety and Instinctual Life,* op. cit. New Introductory Lectures, p. 110.
2   Ibid, (Femininity) p. 112-135.
3   Giovacchini, P. (1982) *A Clinician's Guide to Reading Freud.* Aronson, New York and London, p. 115.
4   Giovacchini, P. op. cit. p. 115.
5   Freud, S. *New Introductory Lectures,* op. cit. p. 112-135.
6   See Winnicott, D., Woods, D. (1984) *Deprivation and Delinquency.* Tavistock, London.
7   Ibid.
8   As attributed to Ian Suttie, see Guntrip, H.(1960) Ego Weakness, Handcore of the Problem, *BR Med Psych,* p. 178.
9   Brown, J. A. A. (1964) *Freud and the Post Freudians.* Penguin, London.
10   Shengold, L. (1979) Child Abuse and Deprivation: Soul Murder. *J Amer Psychoanal Assn. 27,* p. 533-59.
11   Weldon, E. V. (1988) *Mother Madonna Whore, The Idealisation and Denigration of Motherhood.* Free Association Books, London, p. 14, also p. 18.
12   Ibid, p. 5.
13   Ibid, p. 72.
14   Ibid, p. 92.
15   Ibid, p. 92
16   Reid, M. (1992) *Female Sexual Abuse,,* Unpublished Dissertation, Faculty of Social and Health Sciences, University of Ulster.
17   Ibid, p. 43.
18   Ibid, p. 58.
19   Weldon, op. cit. p. 10.
20   Weldon, op. cit. p. 93

21   Shengold, L. (1980) Some reflections on a case of mother/adolescent son incest, *Int J Psychoanal* 61, p. 461-76.

22   Glaser, D. and Frosk, S. (1988) *Child Sexual Abuse.*   Macmillan Education, London.

23   Freud, S. (1975) *Sexual Aetiology of the Neuroses.*   The Complete Works of Sigmund Freud Trans Strachey et al, Vol III, Early Psychoanalytic Publications, Standard Ed. Hogarth Press, London, p. 266.

24   Banning, A. (1989) Mother-Son Incest: Confronting a Prejudice. *Child Abuse and Neglect* 13, 563-570.

25   Lawson, C. (1993) *Mother-Son Sexual Abuse: Rare or Under-Reported* Child Abuse and Neglect 17, 261§-269.

26   Bass, A. (1991) *A Touch for Evil,* Boston Globe Magazine July 7, 12-25.

27   Lewis, D., Malloug, C. and Webb, V. (1989) *Child Abuse, Delinquency and Violent Criminality* in Cicchetti and Carlson (Eds), Child Maltreatment Theory and Research on the Causes and Consequences of Child Abuse and Neglect 707-721, New York: Cambridge.

28   Elliot, M. op. cit.

29   Elliot, M. op. cit.

30   Elliot, M. op. cit.

10 Female sexuality: Approaches towards a theoretical understanding

Our belief in, and insistence upon, feminine and maternal virtuosity is a socially imposed illusion, predicated to protect us from more primitive realities. It represents an attempt to sanitise underlying sexual realities, which disturb. This carries a consequence of psychical conflict which actually serves the cause of perversion. The consequences for individual identity, human relationships, emotional and mental health are enormous.

> Unfortunately what history tells us and what we ourselves have experienced does not speak in this sense but rather justifies a judgement that the belief in the 'goodness' of human nature is one of those evil illusions by which mankind expect their lives to be beautified and made easier while in reality they only cause damage. [1]

Sexuality and gender. A metapsychological analysis

The text to date has established the reality, nature and extent of female sexual abuse of children. This study has also provided evidence to support an "actual" feminine sadistic tendency in the sexual and physical abuse of children, and more generally. While the accounts of sadistic abuse may be regarded as extreme or "pathological", pathological perversion does serve in demonstrating latent, dormant, or repressed strivings, which may be more generally present. As Freud observes "Pathology has always done us the service of making discernible by isolation and exaggeration conditions which would remain concealed in a normal state". [2] A clear deficiency however, is in providing a theoretical or conceptual framework to explain such a "perverse" sadistic disposition in females. One such explanatory approach is offered.

Freud's discussion of "penis envy", [3] in his "Femininity Lecture", [4] established the fact that young girls discover their relative genital deprivation, as a traumatic event. [5] "Her self love is mortified by the comparison with the boy's far superior equipment and in consequence she renounces her masturbatory satisfaction from her clitoris, repudiates her love for the mother and at the same time not infrequently represses a good part of her sexual trends in general".[6] This involves the establishment of a sexual identity based upon mortification, inferiority, jealously and injustice, located in the discovery of their relative "castration".

> Her fate is one of "lack", "atrophy" (of her genitals) and "penis envy" since the penis is the only recognised sex organ of any worth. Therefore she tries to appropriate it for herself, by all the means at her disposal: by her somewhat servile love of the father-husband capable of giving it to her; by her desire of a penis child, preferably male; by gaining access to those cultural values which are still "by right" reserved for males alone and therefore are always masculine etc. Woman lives her desire only as an attempt to possess at long last the equivalent of the male sex organ.
> All of that seems rather foreign to her pleasure, however.[7]

This instance of "male injustice",[8] and "envy and jealousy"[9] toward males, may result in a deep seated hostility toward men (and males), involving aggressive and sadistic feelings toward them (which may be conscious, repressed or unconscious). The genital differences between male and female children, involve the females inferiority, and their "shame".[10] The most common human response to mortification, and being "shamed", is to seek vengeance and retribution from those responsible. (Against those with the means to evoke feelings of shame). This would not usually give rise to passivity, but to aggressive thoughts and feelings. It does not facilitate a masochistic disposition, but one much more located in the sadistic impulse. As Freud observes "shame, which is considered to be a feminine characteristic par excellence but is far more a matter of convention than may be supposed, has as its purpose, we believe, concealment of genital deficiency".[11] Thus when Freud discusses "normal femininity",[12] this may be viewed as a passive position which is occupied to defend against or conceal "aggressive and destructive"[13] masculine traits. Accordingly when Freud writes "The discovery that she is castrated is a turning point in the girl's growth. Three possible lines of development start from it: one leads to sexual inhibition or to neurosis, the second to a change of character in the sense of a masculinity complex, the third, finally, to normal femininity".[14] While this developmental model is accepted, it is being here contend that the relationship, between the masculinity complex and normal femininity is highly interdependent, and not mutually exclusive. Conversely, for the male, the castration complex involves fear, which is associated with sex, and sexuality. In relation to the father the male child is both dependant and defenceless, themes strongly associated with the passive, masochistic position.[15] The female child alternatively perceives an "actual castration", resulting in rage and aggression, impulses much more associated with a drive toward dominance and the sadistic position. For the male, however, there is an imperative to repress and disguise his fear, in defending his truly passive position, projecting and internalising instead, the characteristics expected of the masculine. Conversely the female is required to repress and screen the reality of her aggressiveness and rage and to internalise and project the passive and compliant characteristics associated with femininity. However

93

both these positions, of the masculine, and the feminine, belie underlying psychical realities, and represent essentially the enacted demands both of the external world, and subsequently the super-ego. While societal demands and super-ego function are in the ascendancy in determining the behaviour of the individual, the passive strivings in the male, and the sadistic impulse in the female, will remain repressed.

Accordingly it can be stated that "femininity" may be a defensive response to conceal the secretly experienced masculine (aggressive) impulse, which is, normally, suppressed from consciousness. This may be seen as the central paradox, and inherent conflict, which accounts for the "riddle"[16] of femininity.

> Whatever truth is conceded to each of these standard responses they all miss the crucial point of the perverse strategy. What makes a perversion a perversion is a mental strategy that was one or another social stereotype of masculinity or femininity in a way that deceives the onlooker about the unconscious meanings of the behaviours she or he is observing. ...However, the perversion itself is meant to deceive the woman herself and her audience about the shameful elements in her sexual life.[17]

The shameful elements in feminine sexuality may be located in the possibilities of aggressive and sadistic sexuality, and sexual maternalism.

This is why the mammary glands of the female assume such importance in sexual life, symbolising as they do, sexual maternalism. The sucking, nibbling and biting of the female breasts, which accompanies perhaps most sexual encounters, has a sexual significance, which is in actuality a recreation of the maternal nursery scene. This is an embodiment of male dependence upon the female, and of her sexual, maternal domination over him. This can carry an enormous erotic significance for the female. That the breast can be offered or withdrawn, is the mechanism of maternal power, which continues to carry a significance in sexual power. The sexual fixation with the female breast, is symbolically rooted in the maternal and sexual female supremacy over the male. It may well be that this maternal sexual power over the male, carries such a significance, that it may contribute to the females' relinquishing subsequent social power to the male, divested as this is of sexual content. Accordingly, the female breast provides the opportunity to recreate the circumstance of infantile sexuality which continues to arouse both the male, and the female. For the female child however, the mothers breasts will come to represent her relative inferiority in the sexually competitive relationship with her father. This accounts for the continuing pre-occupation with her breasts, relative to those of other women. As a consequence we have an entire industry dedicated to breast implantation, augmentation and reshaping, which is determined, in the cause of maternal sexuality. The large or perfectly shaped breast is actually a symbol of maternal, sexual power, which affords the means of sexual domination. Hence in the popular press men "pay homage" to the female breast which is deeply associated with infantile sexuality in relation to the original love object, the mother.

There may exist, in the male, an impulse to replicate the sexual infantile relationship with the mother, in adult sexual relations, including his sexualised domination. In this way the passive desires in the male may compliment the sadistic orientation of the female.

Accordingly as we have the possibility of perverse motherhood, or sexual maternalism, we have the certainly of the child's pathological sexual interest in the mother. There may exist a latent or experienced impulse to reinact the sexual nursery scenario in adulthood. Where this is the case, it is an impulse, or compulsion to repeat the circumstance and intensity of maternal and infantile sexuality. The human impulse or compulsion to repeat or replicate past experience is well documented. It is interesting to note the prominence of this theme in accounts of female fantasy.

In reality, this would, at best, only approximate the nature of the sexual intimacy between a mother and her son.

However these are secret realities which must be defended against and hidden, most of all from the feminine and masculine self. While these themes are rarely enacted in adult sexual relations, they may find covert and perverse expression in the nursery. Alternatively the female may be so alarmed by the sexual realities within her, she may successfully deny her masculine strivings, and don a mantle of purity and femininity. In which case she conspires in the denial of the true, sexual self.

In circumstances of "normal femininity" the experienced masculine impulse, or psychical reality, is "taboo".[18] It is disguised, concealed and suppressed to meet the demands of both the super ego and those of the external world. As Freud observes "Taboo is a primeval prohibition forcibly imposed from outside (by some authority) and directed against the most powerful longings to which human beings are subject".[19] However the aggressive masculine impulses experienced by females are subject to the same prohibition as other primitive impulses.

> This desire is promptly met by an external prohibition against carrying out that particular kind of touching. The prohibition is accepted, since it finds support from powerful internal forces, and proves stronger than the instinct which is seeking to express itself in the touching. In consequence, however, of the child's primitive psychical constitution, the prohibition does not succeed in abolishing the instinct. Its only result is to repress the instinct and banish it into unconscious. Both the prohibition and the instinct persist: the instinct because it has only been repressed and not abolished, and the prohibition because, if not ceased. the instinct would force its way through to consciousness and into actual operation. A situation is created which remains undealt with - a psychical fixation - and everything else follows from the continuing conflict between the prohibition and the instinct. [20]

In terms of this model, an internalised moral prohibition may act against the expression of the suppressed sadistic, masculine impulse in females. However in circumstances where this moral, super-ego ascendancy, has been deficient, the impulse may find an outlet. (Examples of this have been extensively provided in this text). Alternatively situational opportunity may provide for a conscious connection with the impulse facilitating its expression and actualisation.

"Penis envy" and the associated sense of deprivation may lead to rage, anger, and a sense of betrayal which may result in a rejection of the mother. The psychical consequences of this are enormous, leading as it commonly does from a change of love object, from the "feminine" mother, to the "masculine" father. This rejection of the mother, and by association the feminine, does not only involve a loss of love, but the conversion of that emotional affect, into hatred. The emotional and psychological consequences of this for a young child are catastrophic, and must call into question the females ability to experience true trust and security in all subsequent relations with the external world. As Freud observes "The turning away from the mother is accompanied by hostility: the attachment to the mother ends in hate".[21] A hate of that kind may become very striking and last all through life: it may be carefully overcompensated later on; as a rule one part of it is overcome while another part persists".[22]

This tendency toward a hatred of the "feminine" mother, and projective identification with the "masculine" father is further consolidated, through the relative under valuation of the female child, when compared with the male. This can be viewed as a gender conspiracy perpetrated upon females, by females, given their preferred, and actual locatedness, within the "masculinity complex".[23]

> The difference in a mother's reaction to the birth of a son or a daughter shows that the old factor of lack of a penis has even now not lost its strength. A mother is only brought unlimited satisfaction by her relation to a son, this is altogether the most perfect the most free from ambivalence of all human relationships. A mother can transfer to her son the ambition which she has been obliged to suppress in herself, and she can expect from him the satisfaction of all that has been left over in her of her masculinity complex. [24]

This represents the great injustice in human affairs, which is based upon sex, and sexual difference. The fact that little boys possess a penis and little girls do not. While mothers' often deeply resent the transfer of her son's affection to another woman, this may be viewed as inevitable. However a mother may be disinclined to give up the special, sexually dominant, nature of her relationship with her son, which gives expression to her masculinity, to another woman. Femininity therefore becomes an absolute requirement and imperative for the female child, which prescribes and constrains her subsequent relationship with the male. In normal circumstances this serves to exclude the possibility of the female's' enacting their aggressive masculine sexuality toward the adult male, who is, the preferred son. Gender socialisation, and subsequent female internalisation of the feminine stereotype, will assure both his social ascendancy, and his sexual primacy, with the 'passive and virtuous' female. This is central to the social and inter-personnel entrapment of the female, and the required abandonment of her masculinity, and true self. The social conspiracy toward the female will involve her individual socialisation, and her treatment in virtually every social context in which she may be placed.

It can be stated therefore, that through giving birth to a son, the mother fulfils her masculine strivings, through producing, and possessing, a penis. At the same time the disproportionate power relationship involves the complete dependence of the male child, and the absolute dominance of the mother. While women, consciously or unconsciously, socially or sexually, strive to approximate this relationship with their husbands, it can scarcely achieve the power and dependency which characterises the mother/son "bond". As Freud observes "Even a marriage is not made secure until the wife has succeeded in making her husband her child as well and in acting as a mother toward him".[25] Further to this, in maintaining the power differential and dominance, it becomes more important for the female to be loved, than to love, in the relationship. As Freud comments "....so that to be loved is a stronger need for them than to love".[26] This provides further evidence of the tendency, or compulsion. in females to strive toward a position of dominance over the male. However this manifests in its purest form between a mother and son, and is, at best, approximated elsewhere.

It is in this identification too that she acquires her attractiveness to a man, whose Oedipus attachment to his mother kindles it into passion. How often it happens however that it is only his son who obtains what he himself aspired to! One gets the impression that man's love and a woman's are a phase apart psychologically.[27]

It could also be contended that penis envy, and its consequence, involving the loss of the original, and most significant "love object", may have entailed a loss of trust in the external world, and in external relationships. It may also be stated that the experience of "abuse" or "castration" at the hands of the all powerful and dominant mother, compels women to 1) resist dependence in all future relationships, 2) assert dominance and power in relationships. The fact that young girls experience the trauma of such a loss, so young, may provide one avenue of explanation as to why females often survive the subsequent death of a spouse, more successfully than males. 1) Given the loss of the most significant love object, their ability to experience love (other than with their sons) may be relatively impaired. 2) Having survived the most catastrophic loss in childhood, they are psychologically more prepared to deal with subsequent loss and trauma. The affective components of this original loss, involve anger and rage, feeding the impulse toward aggression, which coincides with the change of love object (from the feminine mother, to the masculine father). The mother (who is without a penis) is commonly rejected, and a projective identification is formed with the phallic father involving a sexual identification, extending to an identification with the (assumed) male characteristics of physicality, aggressiveness and dominance. These may be viewed as impulses which seek to find expression in a relationship. However given both internal and social censure, role modelling, and convention, these impulses are unlikely to become expressed in male/female sexual, or marital relationships, which require a passive version of femininity. ("But we must be aware in this of underestimating the influence of social customs, which similarly force women into passive situations").[28]

The question remains however, as to whether the socially enforced suppression of the feminine aggressive impulse succeeds in eradicating it, or indeed converts it into a masochistic impulse. This was the view as asserted by Freud.

The suppression of women's aggressiveness which is prescribed for them constitutionally and imposed upon them socially favours the development of powerful masochistic impulses, which succeed, as we know, in binding erotically the destructive trends which have been diverted inwards. [29]

However, upon the basis of the evidence presented in this text, it is contended that this is not always the case. It is equally possible that suppression of aggressiveness, results in the amplification of aggression, which seeks discharge. It is further contended that the socially presented passivity, and masochistic tendencies exist, precisely to defend against, screen, or disguise, the darker reality, the females actual dominant and sadistic disposition. (This view would be supported by the evidence as presented). As Kaplan writes, of the anorectic's perverse strategy "...the anorectic presents herself to the world as a sexless child in a caricature of saint like femininity. Behind her caricature of an obedient, virtuous, clean, submissive good little girl is a most defiant ambitious devious dominating, controlling, virile caricature of masculinity". [30]

Accordingly there may be a tendency to reject passive, masochistic, feminine sexuality, with a sexual identification becoming more located with "masculine" aggressiveness, dominance and sadism. (This is commonly evidenced during the "Tomboy" phase of female development, at which time all things feminine are renounced). A further factor in the consolidation of this tendency is the feminine sense of loss, inferiority and jealously at not possessing a penis. All with all human "inferiority" and jealousy, we strive to possess those things which others have and we do not. This sense of inferiority is normally responded to or defended against, by an impulse or drive to assert relative superiority. "The effect of penis envy has a share, further, in the physical vanity of women, since they are bound to value their charms more highly as a late compensation for their original sexual inferiority". [31] This involves a conscious or unconscious impulse to actually dominate, the male, rather than be dominated by him. This is consolidated by this time, by the affective association between a powerful, dominant love object (mother) and rejection. This may disincline the female to occupy, in psychical reality, the passive and submissive role, assigned to them, as this is powerfully associated with rejection. Consideration should also be given to the "compulsion to repeat" [32] theme, at this point. There may well exist, in some cases, a compulsion to repeat such patterns of relationships, as have been personally experienced. Accordingly, as repetition compulsion, and role reversal operate, as they do, there may be a tendency for the passive "abused" (female) child, to become the dominant, abusing mother. It is interesting to note that this does exist, as a self fulfilling prophecy, and predisposition, in the female child's relation toward the mother.

It may be stated therefore, that the feminine defence against penis envy (and inferiority) impels an impulse to dominate the male, providing for a sexual possession of him, and possession of the penis. In normal circumstances this can be only imperfectively achieved in adult male/female relationships. However the mother/son relationship does allow for both a total dependency, dominance, and "possession of the penis". As Freud observes "Her (the mother's) happiness is great if later on this wish for a baby finds fulfilment in reality, and quite especially so if the baby is a little boy, who brings the longed for penis with him .... In this way the ancient masculine wish for possession of a penis is still faintly visible though the femininity now achieved".[33]

However these sexual themes of dominance, dependency and possession, may be "unconscious" or secret, to be concealed and defended against. Alternatively, as suggested in this text, they may, more commonly than we know, be acted out and expressed perversely or pathologically. As Kaplan comments

> They say that there are more perverse women than the doctors realise. In fact women are just as perverse as men. All doctors have to do is look around them and those odd statistics would even out.[34]

In stark contrast to the female, a boy's dependent relationship with his love object (the mother) remains unchanged and constant. The sexualised desire for the mother, which is experienced from a position of powerlessness, reinforced by the Oedipal fear of the father, galvanises the formative themes of "masculine" sexuality, with sexual desire associated with powerlessness, dependency, and fear. Unlike the psychopathological development of girls these themes remain, without a change of love object. and the "aggression" and "hatred" experienced by females. Crucially the fear experienced by the female, in her castration complex, turns to anger, aggression and hatred, upon the realisation of her "actual" castration. While sexuality in the male continues to be associated in the passive position, the libidinal impulse in the female becomes located in a sexual aggressiveness. The central conflict for the female is that this psychically experienced reality must be denied in expression and repressed as a socially required imperative. However the projective identification for the male child, may remain with the mother, and the perceived passive, feminine, masochistic position.

Through the process of Oedipal amnesia, internalisation and socialisation, these physical realities under-go repression, and may be entirely assigned to the unconscious. However, these are psychical realities, which may strive for recognition in consciousness, and in actual expression. Accordingly the actual sadistic disposition of the female, may have its psychical equivalent, in what may be the actual masochistic tendency in the male. In this event the sexual stereotypes we tend to act out may be defensive, organised and operationalised to mask deeper and darker sexual realities. This may be central to the internal sexual conflict which characterises the human condition involving the suppression and repression of the true self, which becomes transmuted into a "social self", and an identity based largely upon the demands and requirements of the external relational environment.

Sexuality and gender. A psycho-social analysis

It would appear that this selection, and characterisation of gender, owes more to the maintenance of a social order, than to internally experienced psychical realities.

Indeed these internal realities must be sacrificed and repressed in the cause of the social order. Crucially, the social roles and the mechanisms of sexual identification, relate to the distribution of power, and to the maintenance of male power in society. This is a preference not easily given, which has as its origins the female tendency to reject the mother, and to identify centrally within the phallic, masculinity complex. The feminine supremacy of regard for the male child, ensures his legacy of power in social and adult life. The reality is that this is a role, and a fate, more assigned to than seized by the male. Thus in the maternal management of childhood, assertiveness and aggressiveness, and even sexuality are encouraged in the male. However the aggressive and masculine strivings of the female, are disallowed her, and dutifully suppressed, as she becomes trained to enact that version of femininity ascribed to her. The female child is accordingly 'given her place' in the social world, which is determined primarily through conforming to maternal expectations. This involves the abandonment of her aggressive masculine sexuality, and conformity to the requirements of the feminine stereotype. This socially imposed and psychically internalised repression is so pervasive, as the sexual liberation of women, may result in the social liberation of women, which could threaten the entire social status quo.

As Kaplan writes.

> There is some merit to the idea that a female sexuality, more fully explored might be a force that could undermine the social order. This must be so or we would not be so determined to deny, disavow, and repress it. [35]

In this way the sociological, or external realities, inform, or reform, the psychical and instinctual drives, involving to a greater or lesser degree their repression. That is to say that there is imposed upon the feminine child a mediation between the internal world, and the external social expectations of the relational matrix, [36] demanding conformity to the feminine stereotype. As Goffman (1971) observes

> We have to act on someone else's stage and in someone else's play.

> We walk out on a stage that is unfamiliar, we are faced by characters speaking lines that obviously are addressed at us and that expect certain responses but we are unsure what our responses should be and while we are considering it the spotlight is on us, and we can imagine that behind it lies an audience of friends, neighbours and family. [37]

For the female the tensions experienced between the internal (masculine) desire, and external social expectations, normally involve a schism, in which the internally experienced needs and desires are subordinated and repressed.

The externally reflected view of self may be internalised, and colluded with to such an extent that the masculine strivings are denied or disallowed in conscious expression.

> As he develops, the child, in his quest for security tends to stress those traits and aspects of himself which meet with approval and to squelch or deny those aspects which meet with disapproval. Equally the individual develops a concept of himself (self dynamism) which is based upon these perceived appraisals of significant others.[38]

Alternatively, if the female child is unwilling to collude with enacting the required stereotype of femininity, she may be perceived of as bad, and may internalise that external view of who she is.

> The self may be said to be made up of reflected appraisals. If these were chiefly derogatory, as in the case of an unwanted child who was never loved, of a child who had fallen into the hands of foster parents who have no real interest in him as a child; as I say, if the self dynamism is made up of experience which is chiefly derogatory, it will facilitate hostile, disparaging appraisals of other people and it will entertain disparaging and hostile appraisals of itself.[39]

Clearly most female children will avoid the devastating psychological and interpersonal consequences which will be almost inevitably associated with the assertion of the true masculine self, when this so obviously contradicts social expectations.

In such circumstances, the assertion of individuality (and the masculine true self) and self interest, becomes virtually impossible, given the need for acceptance within the social group, or relational matrix. The social persona is accordingly acquired, and internalised, to defend against the true masculine self. Indeed the extent to which femininity is employed by the female, may be, defensively determined in proportion to the perceived, or experienced, threat of the masculine impulse.

> A variety of female impersonations and feminine stereotypes may be used to hide the sexualities and intellectual ambitions that women have learned to fear in themselves. Similarly, nearly every female perversion, disguises vengeful sadistic aims beneath the cloak of feminine masochism... The way I see it, the myth of primary femininity is itself a disguise for the forbidden and frightening masculine ambitions and strivings that "nice" women are not supposed to entertain.[40]

As a consequence there is an inter-dependant relationship between the female's experienced masculinity and the extent to which femininity is defensively employed, to acquire and maintain acceptance and approval.

> Man is by nature committed to social existence, and is therefore inevitably involved in the dilemma between serving his own interests and recognising those of the group to which he belongs. In so far as this

dilemma can be resolved it is resolved by the fact that man's self interest can be best served through commitment to his fellows...Need for positive affect means that each person craves response from his human environment. It may be viewed as hunger, not unlike that for food, but more generalised. Under varying conditions it may be expressed as a desire for contact, for recognition and acceptance, for approval, for esteem or for mastery... As we examine human behaviour, we find that persons not only universally live in social systems which is to say they are drawn together, but also universally act in such ways as to attain the approval of their fellow men.[41]

Clearly this carries equal application for women, and most particularly for women, in the society of women.

The suppression of the aggressive and masculine instincts required in the external world become internalised and structurally incorporated within the super-ego function, resulting in the state of conflict, experienced perhaps, by a majority of females. In this conflict the sexual feminine (aggressive and destructive) strivings of the female tend to be sacrificed, in the social, sexual, and power relationships with the male, to ensure the maternal interest in the supremacy of the male, in preference to the female.

This perhaps affords us a slightly different twist to Freud's wry observation, that a man's, and woman's love, are a generation apart. For while women may consciously resent, at times obsessively, the relative power and status of their male peers, and even husband, they bequeath to their sons the means of status differentiation, which ensures the male ascendancy. This will almost always serve in maintaining the relative inferiority, and oppression, of females in the next generation. Perhaps when the young girl turns away from the mother and develops in hatred for her, she senses her fate, both psychically, and in the circumstance of intimate relationship, which unthinkingly, but conclusively determines her relative inferiority.

Accordingly the young girl conforms to the expectations and requirements of virtuous femininity, perversely designed to enshroud her. In doing so she looses her natural legacy of commonality and equality with the male. In this way the female becomes uncomprehending resigned to her fate, which she accepts, as this is given to her, in love, and with affection. That the primary love for the mother turns to hatred, perhaps justifies the relative maternal distance from the female child. It possibly vindicates the hatred which will be experienced by the female child towards her mother. However the entire ethos of this essentially feminine complex, is pervaded by a pathos, of classical intensity.

Thus as Muslim women centrally contrive in the circumcision of their daughters, Western women collude in the psychological equivalent, in demanding the stereotype of the pure, virtuous, passive, asexual girl and women. The result in both cases, causes physical and psychological distance from experienced feminine sexual potentiality. It further creates a distance from men, central to gender differentiation, and the contrivance of male ascendancy, at both the phychical and psychological levels.

Electra accordingly emerges as a wounded and betrayed child, who rejected in her femininity seeks identification within her masculine self, which will be rigorously denied to her, and within her. While the female child may rebel against her fate, the rebellion will prove unsustainable, at least within the confines of conventional, or normal society.

The central conflict of femininity therefore can be stated as the drive to give expression to the aggressive impulse toward the male, which seeks to dominate him, and the maternal instinct which seeks, and commonly ensures, his gender based elevation. In this conflict, between what are usually the oppositional forces of feminine (aggressive) sexuality and maternalism, the maternal instinct tends to dominate at both the individual and collective social levels. This is, in normal circumstances, an individually imposed, and collectively regulated, conspiracy, which serves to distance women from realising their potential, personally, sexually and socially. It serves, if you will, as a conspiracy against the feminine, centrally perpetrated upon women, by women.

Sexuality and gender. The political dimension

This study has attempted to establish the reality of the feminine masculine and sadistic impulse, by examining female 'perverse sanarios'. It is contended that these are so perverse, largely due to the fact that the masculine desires experienced by women are normally disallowed legitimate expression, and therefore must find expression , perversely. As Kaplan courageously suggests, in this regard. "If her husband does not give her the sexual pleasure she has been anticipating, a woman can get her revenge by using her children for sexual fulfilment." [42] Situational or circumstantial opportunity, defective super-ego development or the strength of the instinctual desires, may all play a part in the females giving expression to the normally repressed masculine impulse. As this impulse is regarded an evaluated as perverse, its expression must involve perversion, as it is denied legitimate discharge, in normal circumstances. Accordingly perceived injustice, envy, jealously, and a required sexual repression, may combine, culminating in the instinctual drive forcing its way into both consciousness and enactment. In these circumstances the perverse erotic potential of the female is likely to exceed that of the male. (As substantially documented in this text).

> When piety and maternal sentiment and wanting and in their place are the strong passions and intensely erotic tendencies, much muscular strength and a superior intelligence for this conception and execution of evil, it is clear that the innocuous semi criminal present in the normal woman must be transformed into a born criminal more terrible than any man.[43]

The injustice encountered by woman, through the required suppression of her true masculine sexuality, makes female perversion both a sexual, and a political act, which has as its justification the sexual and gender conspiracy which otherwise surrounds her. That is, when the females experience of relative physical castration, is compounded through her socially required and regulated emasculation. Female perversion has the potential to be more "passionate" and "erotic" given what may be regarded as the moral justification of gender discrimination and social and sexual oppression.

The infantile and childhood oppression of the female is both introjected into and internalised by her. The parental agency, the super-ego, will subsequently convert the external oppression, into self oppression, with a consequence of repression and conflict, involving the associated symptoms of guilt and neuroticism. The oppressed female will dutifully manifest a "compulsion to repeat" the circumstances of her own oppression, in the management of her own female children. Thus the continuity of inter-generational female oppression, and the maternal interest in the ascendancy of the male child, are assured.

The process of feminine oppression becomes accordingly culturally transmitted, critically, between mother and daughter, fully supported by an approving audience, subconsciously, and perhaps consciously, committed to a maintenance of the social status quo. The cultural and sociological predisposition toward feminine oppression are in due course, complimented and consolidated in psychological and psychical circumstance.

Notes

1   Freud, S. *New Introductory Lectures*, op. cit. p. 104.
2   Ibid, p. 121.
3   Ibid, p. 125.
4   Ibid, p. 112-135.
5   Ibid, p. 125.
6   Irigaray, L. (1980) *Ce Sexe qui n'est pas un*, New French Feminisms, Amherst: University of Massachusetts Press, p. 99
7   Freud, S. *New Introductory Lectures,* op. cit. p. 125.
8   Ibid, p. 126.
9   Ibid, p. 125.
10   Ibid, p. 132.
11   Ibid, p. 132.
12   Ibid, p. 128.
13   Ibid, p. 111.
14   Ibid, p. 126.
15   Ibid, p. 116.
16   Ibid, p. 113.
17   Kaplan, L. op. cit. p. 9-15.
18   Freud, S. *Totem and Taboo,* op. cit. p. 29.
19   Ibid.
20   Ibid, p. 29.
21   Freud, S. *New Introductory Lectures,* op. cit. p. 121.
22   Ibid, p. 121-122.
23   Ibid, p. 130.
24   Ibid, p. 133.
25   Ibid, p. 133-134.
26   Ibid, p. 132.
27   Ibid, p. 116.
28   Ibid, p. 116.

29   Ibid, p. 116
30   Kaplan, L. op. cit. p. 457.
31   Ibid, p. 132.
32   Stevens, R. op. cit. pp. 35, 59.
33   Freud, S. *New Introductory Lectures,* op. cit. p. 128.
34   Kaplan, L. op. cit. p.
35   Kaplan, L. op. cit. p.
36   Goffman, I. (1971) *The Presentation of Self in Everyday Life,* Penquin, London.
37   Goffman, Ibid.
38   Foulkes, S. H.(1986) *Group Analytical Psychotherapy,* Manesfield, London.
39   Yallom, I. D. (1975) *The Theory and Practice of Group Psychotherapy,* Basic Books Inc., New York.
40   Kaplan, L. op. cit. p.
41   Goldschmidt, W. (1963) as quoted by Hamburg D.A. in *Emotions in Perspective of Human Evaluation* in, Knapp, P. (Ed.) *Expressions of Emotions in Man.* International Universities Press, New York.
42   Kaplan, L. op. cit. p. 200.
43   Lombroso, C. and Ferris, W.(1899) *The Female Offender,* Appleton, New York, p. 151.

11 Conclusion

This paper has traced the "inevitably" [1] of maternal sensuality/sexuality upon the basis of the Freudian, and other literature. It has examined the repression of sexuality, and female sexuality in particular, from historical medical approaches, [2] to the practice of the surgical desexualisation of females. [3] Psychological and sociological modalities of sexual repression, and regulation, were also considered and assessed. [4]

Accounts of female fantasy were drawn from the literature, and these pointed (if only in fantasy) to an internal reality of a sadistic female perversion (or perverse impulses). [5] Clinical case histories were documented, and these further asserted, in clinical reality, evidence of a perverse female, sadistic impulse. [6] Empirical research was presented and analysed which established an incidence of "perverse motherhood" or "sexual maternalism". While this was encountered quite frequently by some of the psychotherapist respondents with small caseloads, significantly, it was not by others, even by those with caseloads in the thousands. Accounts from the survivors of female sexual abuse were considered at length, which provided graphic evidence attesting to both sexual maternalism, and the sexualised impulse manifest in sadistically abusive female behaviours. [7] The prevalence of child sexual abuse by females was considered upon the basis of the literature, particularly in infant nursery contexts. [8] Penultimately models of maternalism, and their inferred consequences were outlined, ranging from "moral maternalism", to sexual, or "sexualised maternalism". Finally, as all the presented material was so oppositional to the social stereotype of the feminine, and the maternal, a metapsychological analysis was advanced to explain the psychopathology of sexual maternalism, and the sadistic impulse in women.

In writing this paper one was very aware of Freud's "inevitable fate", when he brought unpalatable sexual realities to professional, and public attention. [9] Reality can be very disturbing, while the myths and stereotypes with which we surround ourselves, provide comfort and reassurance. However they have a more covert function, which is to mask and deflect internal realities, behind the acquired social persona and facade. Clearly some women do internalise the requirements of the feminine stereotype, to a point where they become a true caricature of the stereotype. Other women however, experience realities which are more internally, than socially, driven.

In these circumstances the sadistic impulse will tend to be in the ascendancy, and sexual maternalism may well be one consequence. Whether this involves a small proportion of women, or a majority, is a matter of speculation. However it should be the focus of rigorous social, scientific, and therapeutic research. One thing is certain, if we look for evidence to justify our surmises in this regard, it will be there. The only questions are those of degree and prevalence. As Louis Pasteur commented "where observation is concerned, chance favours only the prepared mind".[10] Our resistance to accepting, or even exploring, the primitive realities, which characterise the human condition, has been a major impediment in our understanding, to date, of the real nature of female sexuality.

In contemporary society feminine (aggressive) sexuality tends either to undergo repression (at great psychical cost), or to become expressed perversely, typically in perverse motherhood. Both these responses to internally experienced drives and impulses are the product of social attitudes and expectations which normally disallow women a legitimate expression of their true sexuality in social and adult relationships. The sexual inhibitions and proscriptions upon the female exist, to ensure the sexual primacy of the male, and the relative passivity of the female. This is a socially constructed reality, which is totally oppositional to the psychical and biological reality, where the sexual primacy is demonstrably feminine. If we are not prepared to exercise a great deal more tolerance and liberalism toward sexuality in general (where we are all hypocrites), and female sexuality in particular, women and children will continue to pay the price, in the currency of mental health, and sexual abuse. However, as Kaplan correctly observed, the implications of the sexual liberation of women are revolutionary,[11] and will be resisted, perhaps most of all by women. Accordingly impeded sexual aggressiveness in women, may continue to cause "grave injury".[12] in maintaining both the status quo, and male ascendancy.

Notes

1   Freud, S. (1975) *Three Essays on the Theory of Sexuality Vol. VII (1911-13)* Ed. Strachey, J. et al, Hogarth Press, London, pp. 124-245.

2   Ibid, p. 36.

3   Freud, S. (1975) *New Introductory Lectures Vol. XXII (1936)* Ed Strachey, J. et al, Hogarth Press, London.
See Stevens, R. (1983) Freud and Psychoanalysis, An Exposition and Appraisal. Open University Press, Milton Keynes, p. 57.
Also Brown, D. and Pedder, J. (1991) *Introduction to Psychotherapy,* Routledge, London, p. 33.

4   Stevens, R. op. cit. p. 57.

5   Brown, D. and Pedder, J. op. cit. p. 33.
Kline, P. (1984) *Psychology and Freudian Theory,* Methuen, London, p. 44.
Also Storr, A. (1989) *Freud*, Oxford University Press, Oxford, p. 18.

6   Jahoda, M. (1977) *Freud and the Dilemmas of Psychology*, Hogarth Press, London.

7   Freud, S. (1975) *Pre-psychoanalytic Publications and Unpublished Draft* (1886-89) Ed. Strachey, J. et al, Hogarth Press, London.

8   Giovacchini, P. (1982) *A Clinicians Guide to Reading Freud*, Aronson, New York, p. 115.

9   Freud, S. *New Introductory Lectures*, op. cit. p. 120.

10   Freud, S. *New Introductory Lectures*, op. cit. p. 120.

11   Kaplan, L. Female Perversions, op. cit.

12   Freud, S. *New Introductory Lectures*, op. cit.

Bibliography

Badcock, C. (1992) *Essential Freud*, 2nd Ed, Blackwell, Oxford.

Banning, A. (1989) Mother-Son Incest: Confronting a Prejudice. *Child Abuse and Neglect* 13, 563-570.

Barry, K. *Female Sexual Slavery*, New York University Press, New York.

Bass, A. (1991) A Touch for Evil, *Boston Globe Magazine* July 7, 12-25.

Beauvoir, S.de. (1972) *The Second Sex*, translated and edited by H M Ponshley, Penguin, London.

Becker, H. (1963) *Outsiders, Studies in the Sociology of Deviance*, Glencoe Free Press, New York.

Becker, H. (1968) *The Other Side, Perspectives on Deviance*, New York Free Press.

Bloch, I. (1938) *Sexual Life in England Past and Present*, London.

Brown, J A C. (1964) *Freud and the Post Freudians*, Penguin, London.

Brown, D. and Peddar, J. (1991) *Introduction to Psychotherapy*, Routledge, London.

Bullough, V. L. (1976) *Sexual Variance in Society and History*, University of Chicago Press, Chicago.

Child Sex Abuse, (1981) *National Incidence Study*, Washington DC.

Clark, D. S. (1965) *What Freud Really Said*, Penguin, London.

Cloward, R. and Ohlin (1960) *Delinquency and Opportunity*, The Free Press, New York.

Douglas, J. D. et al; (eds) (1980) *Introduction to the Sociologies of Everyday Life*, Allyn and Bacon Inc, Boston.

Durkheim, E. (1964) *Division of Labour and Society*, Free Press of Glencoe, New York, Vol 3.

Edwards, D. G. (1982) Existential Psychotherapy, *The Process of Caring,* Gardner Press, New York.

Elliott, M. (1993) Female Sexual Abuse of Children, *The Ultimate Taboo,* Longman, Essex.

Faller, K. (1987) Women Who Sexually Abuse Children. *Violence and Victims*.

Finkelhor, D. and Russell, D. (1984) Women as Perpetrators: Review of the Evidence; In Finkelhor D (Ed). *Child Sexual Abuse, New Theory and Research,* Beverley Hills, CA, Sage.

Fisher, G. (1990) Conference Paper: Treatment of Sexual Abusers 4/6 October, Toronto.

Freud, A. (1968) *The Ego and Mechanisms of Defence,* J Strachey et al, (eds) Hogarth, London.

Freud, S. (1975) *An Infantile Neurosis and Other Works,* J Strachey et al, (eds) Hogarth, London.

Freud, S. (1975) *Early Psychoanalytical Publications,* J Strachey et al, (eds) Vol. III (1893-99) Hogarth Press, London.

Freud, S. (1975) *New Introductory Lectures of Psychoanalysis and Other Works,* J. Strachey et al, (eds) Vol XXII (1932-36), Hogarth Press, London.

Freud, S. (1975) *Collected Papers* Vol I J Strachey et al, (eds) Hogarth Press, London.

Freud, S. (1975) *A Case of Hysteria and Three Essays on Sexuality and Other Works* Vol VII 1901-1905. Strachey et al, (eds) Hogarth Press, London.

Freud, S. (1975) *Femininity,* Works of Sigmund Freud (1932-36). Strachey et al, (eds) Hogarth Press, London.

Freud, S. (1975) *Totem and Taboo and Other Works* J Strachey et al, (eds) Vol XIII 1913-14. Hogarth Press, London, pp. 1-7.

Freud, S. (1975) *Pre Psychoanalytical Publications and unpublished Drafts,* Vol. I (1886-99), J Strachey et al, (eds) Hogarth Press, London.

Giovacchini, P. (1982) *A Clinician's Guide to Reading Freud, Further Remarks of the Defence of the Neuro-psychoses,* Aronson, New York and London.

Glaser, D. and Frosh, S. (1988) *Child Sexual Abuse,* Macmillan Education, London.

Guntrip, H. (1960) Ego Weakness, Hardcore of the Problem, *Br Med Psych.*

Hawkins, J. Tiederman (1975) *The Creation of Deviance,* Merrill, Columbas, Ohio.

Irigaray, L. (1980) *Ce Sexe qui n'est pas un, New French Feminisms,* Amherst: University of Massachusetts Press.

Jahoda, M. (1977) *Freud and the Dilemmas of Psychology,* Hogarth Press, London.

Jung, C. G. (1971) *Four Archetypes,* Routledge, Kegan and Paul, London.

Jung, C. G. (1972) *The Collected Works,* ed. Read, Fordan and Adler, Vol VI Psychological Types, Routledge, Kegan and Paul, London.

Kaplan, L. J. (1993) *Female Perversions,* Penguin, London.

Kincaid, J. (1993) *Child Loving. The Erotic Child and Victorian Culture.* Routledge, London.

Kitchener, A. T. (1812) *Letters on Marriage,* Vol I, Chapple, London.

Kline, P. (1984) *Psychology and Freudian Theory,* An Introduction. Methuen and Co, London.

Kraft-Ebing, R. (1886) *Psychopathis Sexualis,* Stuttgart.

La Fontaine, (1990) *Child Sexual Abuse,* Basil Blackwell Inc, Oxford.

Lawson, C. (1993) *Mother-Son Sexual Abuse: Rare or Under-Reported Child Abuse and Neglect* 17.

Leedings, (1982) *Child Care Manual for Social Workers*, 4th Ed, Butterworth, London.

Lemert, E. (1967) *Human Deviance, Social Problems and Social Control*, Prentice Hall, New York.

Lees, S. (1993) *Sugar and Spice, Sexuality and Adolescent Girls*. Penguin, London.

Lewis, D., Malloug, C. and Webb, V. (1989) Child Abuse, Delinquency and Violent Criminality in Cicchetti and Carlson (eds), *Child Maltreatment Theory and Research on the Causes and Consequences of Child Abuse and Neglect* 707-721, New York: Cambridge.

Lindzey, G. (1967) Some Remarks Concerning Incest, The Incest Taboo and Psychoanalytic Theory, *American Psychologist*.

Lock, M. (1990) Personal Communication recorded in La Fontaine, op. cit.

Mason, M. (1994) *The Making of Victorian Sexuality*, Oxford University Press, Oxford.

Medical Times 21 (1850) London.

Meiselman, K. (1979) *Incest. A Psychological Study of causes and effects with treatment recommendations*, Jossey Bass, London.

Moll, A. (1912) *The Sexual Life of the Child*, translated by Dr M Eden Paul, Berlin.

Morris, D. (1967) *The Naked Ape*, Corgi Books.

Observer, (1.3.1992) *News Section*, Child Sexual Abuse by Females.

Olson, E. A. (1981) *Socio-economic and psycho-cultural context of child abuse in Turkey* in J E Corbin (Ed), Child Abuse and Neglect, Cross Cultural Perspectives, University of California Press, Berkeley.

Reid, M. (1992) *Female Sexual Abuse*. Unpublished Dissertation, Faculty of Social and Health Sciences, University of Ulster.

Research Team (The), QUB/RVH,(1992) *Child Sexual Abuse in NI*. A Research Study of Incidence, Greystone, Antrim.

Rousseau, J. J. (1954) *Confessions*, Penguin Books, London.

Sartre, J. P. (1962) *Existential Psychoanalysis*, H Regency, Chicago.

Seebohm Report (1968) *Report to the Committee on Local Authority and Allied Personal Social Services*, Cmnd 3703, London: HMSO.

Shengold, L. (1979) Child Abuse and Deprivation. Soul Murder, *J Amer Psychoanal Assn 27*.

Shengold, L. (1983) Some Reflections on a case of mother/adolescent incest, *Int J Psychoanal* 61.

Stevens, R. (1983) *Freud and Psychoanalysis. An Exposition and Appraisal*, Open University Press, Milton Keynes.

Stekel, W. Sadism and Masochism. *The Psychology of Hatred and Cruelty*, translated by Louis Brink Liveright, New York.

Storr, A. (1989) *Freud*, Oxford University Press, Oxford.

Sutherland, E. and Cressey, D. (1971) *Learning and Transmitting Criminal Behaviour*. The Criminal in Society, ed. L Radzinowcz, M Wolfgang, Backs Books Inc, USA.

Sutherland, E. and Cressey, D. (1974) in *Principles of Criminology*, 9th Ed, Lippincott, Philadelphia.

Tannenbaum, F. (1938) *Crime and the Community*, Columbia University Press, New York.

Tissot, S. A. D. (1758) *Dissertatio de Febribue Bilbliois*, Lausanne, Switzerland: Marci-Mic Bousquet.

Trepper, T. S. (1990) In Celebration of the Case Study. *Journal of Family Psycho Therapy* 1(1) 5-13.

Vallery-Radot, R. (1900) *La Vie de Pasteur* Ch.4. (Source: The Oxford dictionary of quotations, New edition 1992, BCA, London. No further detail given).

Woolf, V. (1929) *A Room of One's Own*, Harcourt, London.

Addendum

Author's Request

As part of the on-going research in this area, the author, and his associates, would like to establish contact with individuals who can locate themselves within the following categories:

1. Men or women who have been sexually abused by their mother, or other female, during childhood.

2. Mothers or females who feel at risk of abusing.

3. Men who are in a physically or sexually abusive relationship with a woman (wife or partner).

4. Women who experience, or act upon, a (sadistic) aggressive component in their sexuality.

Confidentiality will be scrupulously observed, and any subsequently published material anonomised.

If you are in a position to help in this sensitive area of research please contact Colin Crawford, in the first instance, @ 01232 365131 or by letter to:

Faculty of Social and Health Sciences and Education
University of Ulster
Shore Road
Newtownabbey
BT37 OQB